Manual de actividades que a<

Sol y viento

Beginning Spanish
Second Edition
Volume 1
Lección preliminar–Lección 5B

Bill VanPatten

Texas Tech University

Michael J. Leeser

Florida State University

Gregory D. Keating

San Diego State University

Mc Graw Hill

Boston   Burr Ridge, IL   Dubuque, IA   Madison, WI   New York   San Francisco   St. Louis
Bangkok   Bogotá   Caracas   Kuala Lumpur   Lisbon   London   Madrid   Mexico City
Milan   Montreal   New Delhi   Santiago   Seoul   Singapore   Sydney   Taipei   Toronto

Higher Education

Manual de actividades que acompaña
Sol y viento
Beginning Spanish
Second Edition
Volume 1

Published by McGraw-Hill, an imprint of The McGraw-Hill Companies, Inc., 1221 Avenue of the Americas, New York, NY 10020. Copyright © 2009 by The McGraw-Hill Companies, Inc. All rights reserved. No part of this publication may be reproduced or distributed in any form or by any means, or stored in a database or retrieval system, without the prior written consent of The McGraw-Hill Companies, Inc., including, but not limited to, in any network or other electronic storage or transmission, or broadcast for distance learning.

This book is printed on acid-free paper.

1 2 3 4 5 6 7 8 9 0 QPD QPD 0 9 8

ISBN 978-0-07-334289–4

MHID 0-07-334289–0

Editor-in-chief: *Michael J. Ryan*
Publisher: *William R. Glass*
Executive editor: *Christa Harris*
Director of development: *Scott Tinetti*
Development editor: *Pennie Nichols*
Marketing manager: *Jorge Arbujas*
Production editor: *Mel Valentín*
Production supervisor: *Louis Swaim*
Photo research coordinator: *Nora Agbayani*
Freelance photo researcher: *Judy Mason*
Compositor: *Aptara—York*
Typeface: *10/12 Palatino*
Printer and binder: *Quebecor World Printing, Dubuque*

Photo credits: *Page 17* PhotoDisc/Getty Images; *33* Sexto Sol/Getty Images; *47* Odyssey/Frerck/Chicago; *63* Stephane Cardinale/Corbis; *77* Courtesy of Nancie King-Mertz; *95* Brian Hagiwara/FoodPix/Getty Images; *111* AP/Wide World Photos; *125* Stephanie Colasanti/Corbis; *141* PhotoDisc/Getty Images; *157* Bettmann/Corbis

www.mhhe.com

Contents

Notes to the Students

Welcome to the *Manual de actividades* to accompany *Sol y viento*, Second Edition, Volume 1! The *Manual* is a combined workbook and laboratory manual with additional listening, writing, and pronunciation activities. This volume contains activities related to the vocabulary and grammar presented in the **Lección preliminar** through **Lección 5B** of your textbook. It also contains practice with the story line from the *Sol y viento* film from the **Prólogo** to **Episodio 5**.

- Each lesson of the *Manual* contains a **Primera parte, Segunda parte,** and **Tercera parte** that correspond to the same sections in your textbook. Within each of these sections, you will find a set of activities labeled **Vocabulario** and a set labeled **Gramática,** each of which provide additional written and aural practice with the material presented in the textbook.

- Each string of activities within a **Vocabulario** and **Gramática** section ends with a note that directs you to complete a particular activity that will be turned in later. These activities are called **¡Acción!** and appear at the end of the lesson. These activities are open-ended and allow you to demonstrate your ability to use the vocabulary and grammar presented in meaningful contexts. The section of **¡Acción!** activities is designed such that once a lesson is completed, you can tear out the section and turn it in to your instructor for review and evaluation.

  In general, when you complete a **Vocabulario** section in the textbook, you should then complete the corresponding section in the *Manual* and the **¡Acción!** activity that concludes it. As you complete a **Gramática** section in the textbook, you should then complete the corresponding section in the *Manual* and **¡Acción!** activity that concludes it. After completing all **Vocabulario** and **Gramática** sections, you will have completed all **¡Acción!** activities and may turn them in.

- At the end of every "A" lesson (e.g., **Lección 1A, Lección 2A,** and so forth) is a special listening section called **¡A escuchar!** Although the vocabulary and grammar sections also include listening activities, they are designed for learning and practice of the particular target items in those sections. In contrast, the **¡A escuchar!** sections work on listening skills in a similar way that reading skills are worked on in the **¡A leer!** sections of your textbook. In these **¡A escuchar!** sections, you will find both pre- and post-listening activities. In addition, particular listening strategies are highlighted and developed (e.g., recognizing cognates, guessing words in context, and so forth). The **¡A escuchar!** activities all revolve around two people, Roberto and Marisela, as they have a conversation about the characters or plot in the *Sol y viento* film. Thus, a byproduct of these listening activities is the modeling of language on how to express opinions, make comments, and so forth—language that is very useful for you as you discuss the film in class.

- At the end of every "B" lesson (e.g., **Lección 1B, Lección 2B,** and so forth) are writing activities called **Para escribir.** These activities focus on having you comment on, describe, and otherwise write about the *Sol y viento* film. Each **Para escribir** section contains three subsections: **Antes de escribir** (pre-writing activities), **A escribir** (drafting activities), and **Al entregar la composición** (peer editing and final draft activities). The idea here is to get you to first think about what you want to say and organize your thoughts. You then draft and rewrite as you see fit and are encouraged to get feedback from others. Finally, you will edit your draft, check your work for correct usage of certain grammar points, and then turn in a polished composition to your instructor.

- To do the listening activities (indicated with a headphones icon in the margin), you must listen to the Laboratory Audio Program to accompany *Sol y viento*. This program is available for purchase on a set of audio CDs and is also available on the Online Learning Center **(www.mhhe.com/solyviento2).**

- All activities in the *Manual* have right and wrong answers so that you can check your work as you go. The Answer Key contains the answers to the non-audio-based activities. The answers to most audio-based activities are given right on the audio program itself. Some audio-based activities also have answers that are included in the Answer Key; these are signaled by an icon (▲).

¡Aquí estamos!

OBJETIVOS

IN THIS PRELIMINARY LESSON, YOU WILL CONTINUE TO PRACTICE:

■ how to greet people and make introductions in Spanish

■ the Spanish alphabet

■ the verb **ser** and some of its basic uses

■ talking about courses and majors

■ articles and the gender and number of nouns

■ naming common objects and people in the classroom

■ the verb **estar** and one of its basic uses

Vocabulario

Me llamo...

Introductions

Actividad A Presentaciones

The following statements represent what people might say when meeting for the first time. Put them in the correct order, from 1 to 5.

_____ Igualmente. Carlos, ¿cuál es tu apellido?

_____ Es la doctora Ramírez.

_____ Es Montero. ¿Cómo se llama el profesor?

_____ Hola, Inés. Me llamo Carlos. Mucho gusto.

_____ Hola. Me llamo Inés Delgado.

 ### Actividad B Los saludos

Listen to each statement or question and circle the best response. You will hear each statement or question twice.

> MODELO: (*you hear*) Hola, me llamo Ernesto. ¿Y tú?
> (*you see*) **a.** De México. **b.** Igualmente. **c.** Me llamo Juan.
> (*you circle*) ⓒ Me llamo Juan.

1. **a.** Igualmente.   **b.** Se llama Elena.   **c.** Me llamo Ana.

2. **a.** Diego.   **b.** De California.   **c.** Es Martínez.

3. **a.** Mucho gusto.   **b.** Mi nombre es Elena.   **c.** ¿Cómo te llamas?

4. **a.** Se llama Marta.   **b.** Es Goldstein.   **c.** Mucho gusto.

5. **a.** Raúl.   **b.** Mucho gusto.   **c.** Es Jones.

6. **a.** Se llama Miguel.   **b.** Es Fernández.   **c.** Mucho gusto.

 Go to page 15 to complete ¡**Acción! 1.**

PRONUNCIACIÓN: Las vocales (*Vowels*)

Paso 1 Compared to English vowel sounds, Spanish vowels are fewer in number, do not exhibit great dialectal differences, and are more consistent in pronunciation. There are five vowels in Spanish: **a, e, i, o,** and **u.** Compared to English, Spanish vowels are shorter and more tense, and they do not experience *rounding* or *flattening* as English vowels do. Take the example of the Spanish word **no.** In English, the vowel is longer and ends in a *w* sound (this is an example of *rounding* because to make the *w* sound, you round and close your lips). The vowel in Spanish **no,** however, is shorter without rounding.

Paso 2 Listen to the pronunciation of "no," first in English, then in Spanish.

English: no   no   no

Spanish: no   no   no

Paso 3 In addition, Spanish does not *reduce* vowels. In English, it is typical for speakers to use an *uh* sound when vowels have weak stress. For example, the word *constitution* is generally spoken with two *uh* sounds in regular speech: con-*stuh*-too-*shuhn.* This *reduction* of vowels never happens in Spanish. Spanish vowels are always consistently pronounced.

Paso 4 Listen to the pronunciation of each word. Repeat after the speaker, trying to pronounce the vowels as best as you can. Don't worry about the meanings of the words; just focus on their pronunciation.

    1. **a:** para   carta   papa

    2. **e:** Pepe   trece   ese

    3. **i:** mi   ti   fui

    4. **o:** como   poco   somos

    5. **u:** tú   Lulu   guru

Paso 5 Listen to the pronunciation of each phrase. Repeat after the speaker, trying to pronounce the vowels as best as you can. Avoid using the *uh* sound when pronouncing the vowels in boldface.

    1. muchas gracias
    2. las ciencias
    3. una profesora de filosofía
    4. una mochila
    5. la velocidad

Gramática

Soy de México.   **Introduction to ser**

 Actividad C ¿Cómo se escribe? (*How do you write it?*)*

▲ You will hear the names of several countries spelled in Spanish. Listen and write the name of each country in the corresponding blank. **Note:** You may wish to review the Spanish alphabet, printed on the inside front cover of your textbook, before beginning this activity.

1. _____   5. _____

2. _____   6. _____

3. _____   7. _____

4. _____   8. _____

Actividad D ¿De dónde eres?

Listen to each statement and write the letter of the famous person to whom it refers. You will hear each statement twice.

1. _____   5. _____   **a.** Gloria Estefan
                             b. Nelson Mandela
2. _____   6. _____   **c.** Vladimir Putin
                             d. Celine Dion
3. _____   7. _____   **e.** Julio Iglesias
                             f. Jacques Chirac
4. _____   8. _____   **g.** Luciano Pavarotti
                             h. Salma Hayek

Actividad E ¿Quién es?

As you know, subject pronouns in Spanish are not always expressed in sentences. Circle the subject pronoun that corresponds to each of the following sentences.

1. Son de Texas.   **a.** yo   **b.** ellas   **c.** nosotros   **d.** vosotras

2. Es mi profesora favorita.   **a.** tú   **b.** ellos   **c.** ella   **d.** nosotros

3. ¿De dónde eres?   **a.** yo   **b.** tú   **c.** él   **d.** ellas

4. Somos de Panamá.   **a.** tú   **b.** ellos   **c.** vosotras   **d.** nosotros

5. Soy chicana.   **a.** yo   **b.** tú   **c.** ella   **d.** vosotras

6. ¿Sois españoles?   **a.** tú   **b.** él   **c.** nosotras   **d.** vosotros

Go to page 15 to complete ¡Acción! 2.

---

*The answers to most audio-based activities can be heard on the audio program. The triangle symbol next to activities that are audio-based indicates that the answers are found in the Answer Key at the back of this *Manual*.

PRONUNCIACIÓN: Los acentos

Paso 1 Identifying stressed syllables in Spanish is relatively easy. Words that end in a vowel or the consonants **-n** and **-s** are stressed on the next to the last syllable. Listen and repeat the following words. The stressed syllable appears in bold.

1. mo**chi**la (*backpack*)
2. profe**so**ra
3. en**can**tado (*pleased to meet you*)
4. e**xa**men
5. ape**lli**do
6. **e**res

Paso 2 Words that end in consonants other than **-n** or **-s** are stressed on the last syllable. Listen and repeat the following words. The stressed syllable appears in bold.

1. libe**ral**
2. natu**ral**
3. liber**tad**
4. universi**dad**
5. regu**lar**
6. fa**vor**

Paso 3 Words that do not follow the rules in **Pasos 1** and **2** have a written accent mark to indicate where to place the stress. Compare the following pairs of words. Listen and repeat each word. Again, the stressed syllable appears in bold.

1. **e**res   es**tás** (*you are*)
2. **cla**ses   in**glés**
3. e**xa**men   e**xá**menes
4. co**lor**   **dó**lar
5. ex**pli**co (*I explain*)   **nú**mero
6. prac**ti**co (*I practice*)   **prác**tico (*practical*)
7. je**rez** (*sherry*)   **lá**piz (*pencil*)

Paso 4 Now pronounce the following words using the rules you've learned. When you hear the number, say the corresponding word. Then listen to the pronunciation of each word and compare what you hear with your own pronunciation.

1. aquí (*here*)
2. psicología
3. historia
4. actitud (*attitude*)
5. hombre (*man*)
6. mujer (*woman*)
7. plástico
8. bolígrafo (*pen*)
9. teléfono
10. policía
11. dócil
12. practican (*they practice*)

Vocabulario

Las materias   **School Subjects**

Actividad A   Categorías

Circle the general area to which each school subject belongs.

1. el español

   a. el comercio   **b.** las humanidades y las artes   **c.** las comunicaciones

2. la historia

   a. el comercio   **b.** las ciencias naturales   **c.** las ciencias sociales

3. la biología

   a. las ciencias naturales   **b.** la informática   **c.** las ciencias sociales

4. la contabilidad

   a. las ciencias naturales   **b.** el comercio   **c.** las comunicaciones

5. los estudios latinos

   a. el comercio   **b.** los estudios interdepartamentales   **c.** las ciencias naturales

6. la administración de empresas

   a. el comercio   **b.** las humanidades y las artes   **c.** las ciencias sociales

7. la antropología

   a. las ciencias naturales   **b.** las ciencias sociales   **c.** las comunicaciones

8. la física

   a. las ciencias naturales   **b.** las ciencias sociales   **c.** la informática

Actividad B   Más (*More*) categorías

Listen to each description, then circle the corresponding school subject.

1. **a.** la biología   **b.** la literatura   **c.** la física

2. **a.** la economía   **b.** la química   **c.** la música

3. **a.** el alemán   **b.** la antropología   **c.** la astronomía

4. **a.** la psicología   **b.** la contabilidad   **c.** la astronomía

5. **a.** el arte   **b.** los estudios sobre el género **c.** la filosofía

6. **a.** la contabilidad   **b.** las matemáticas   **c.** la informática

7. **a.** los estudios latinos   **b.** las comunicaciones   **c.** la administración de empresas

8. **a.** la economía   **b.** la contabilidad   **c.** las matemáticas

Actividad C Descripciones

Match the names with the corresponding subjects.

1. _____ Picasso, da Vinci, Rodin

2. _____ Sócrates, Platón, Aristóteles

3. _____ Shakespeare, Cervantes, Allende

4. _____ Mozart, Bach, Beethoven

5. _____ Freud, Jung

6. _____ Galileo, Copérnico

7. _____ Darwin

8. _____ Dell, Gates, Jobs

a. la astronomía
b. la literatura
c. la biología
d. la psicología
e. el arte
f. la informática
g. la filosofía
h. la música

 Go to page 15 to complete ¡Acción! 3.

PRONUNCIACIÓN: b/v, d/g

Paso 1 In Spanish, the letters **b** and **v** represent the exact same sound, whereas in English they are different. For example, *bat* and *vat* are two different words in English. If you say the words out loud and stop yourself as you say the initial consonants, you will notice that your lips and teeth are in different positions for each consonant.

The letters **b** and **v** in Spanish are both pronounced like an English *b* at the beginning of a sentence, after a pause, and after nasal consonants like **m** and **n**. Between vowels, **b** and **v** are pronounced like no comparable sound in English. The lips come together like a *b* sound, but air escapes. This pronunciation probably sounds like an English *v* to you, but it is not.

Paso 2 Listen as the **b** and **v** sounds shift, depending on their position.

base

Cuba

va (*he/she goes*)

cava (*champagne*)

Paso 3 The letters **d** and **g** in Spanish are pronounced similarly to their English counterparts at the beginning of words, after pauses, and after nasal consonants. Like **b** and **v**, however, their pronunciation changes between vowels as air is allowed to pass freely between the lips.

Paso 4 Listen to the pronunciation of the following words.

de

cede (*seat* [*gov.*])

gol

vagón

Paso 5 Listen carefully and repeat each set of words. Try to imitate the correct pronunciation of the consonants in boldface.

1. **d**ías, buenos **d**ías
2. **D**aniel, tú y **D**aniel
3. **d**a, na**d**a
4. **g**ato, mi **g**ato
5. **g**racias, muchas **g**racias
6. **b**ien, muy **b**ien
7. **v**einte, y **v**einte

Gramática

El cálculo y las matemáticas   **Naming Things: Articles, Gender, and Number**

 Actividad D   ¿Es típico?

You will hear two options for completing each of the following partial sentences. Select the correct option and then indicate whether the entire sentence represents a typical situation or not.

> MODELO: (*you see*)   En una mochila típica hay unos...
>
> (*you hear*)   **a.** libros   **b.** sillas
>
> (*you select and say*)   libros, y es típico

1. En una sala de clase típica, hay unas...
   ¿Es típico o no?
2. En una mochila típica, hay por lo menos (*at least*) un...
   ¿Es típico o no?
3. En una sala de clase típica, hay unos...
   ¿Es típico o no?
4. En una mochila típica, hay unas...
   ¿Es típico o no?
5. En una sala de clase típica, hay unos...
   ¿Es típico o no?

Actividad E En el consultorio del médico (*doctor's office*)

First, circle the correct item for each article. Then check **sí** or **no** to indicate whether that item is normally found in a pediatrician's waiting room.

					SÍ	NO
1.	unos				☐	☐
	a. lápiz	**b.** escritorios	**c.** mujer	**d.** sillas		
2.	la				☐	☐
	a. sillas	**b.** libro	**c.** hombre	**d.** calculadora		
3.	las				☐	☐
	a. chicas	**b.** chicos	**c.** mochila	**d.** estudiante		

						SÍ	NO

4. una

a. mujeres   **b.** computadora   **c.** bolígrafos   **d.** escritorio   □   □

5. los

a. hombres   **b.** mochilas   **c.** estudiante   **d.** sillas   □   □

6. un

a. lápiz   **b.** chica   **c.** mochila   **d.** estudiantes   □   □

7. unas

a. libros   **b.** silla   **c.** escritorio   **d.** mujeres   □   □

8. el

a. cafetería   **b.** chicos   **c.** libro   **d.** mujer   □   □

 Go to page 16 to complete **¡Acción! 4.**

🎧 PRONUNCIACIÓN: p, t, k

Paso 1 Unlike in English, the sounds represented by **p, t,** and **k** are not *aspirated* in Spanish. What does it mean to aspirate? If you hold a small strip of paper in front of your lips and say the following words in English, you will see the paper move as you produce a puff of air.

pope

toad

kite

cat

This is aspiration. Spanish does not make this puff.

Paso 2 Listen to the lack of aspiration for the **p, t,** and **k** sounds in each of the following words. Repeat each word and imitate what you hear as best as you can.

1. papá
2. para (*for*)
3. porque (*because*)
4. todavía
5. tú
6. cómo
7. cuál
8. qué

Vocabulario

En la sala de clase

Classroom Objects

 Actividad A Los objetos

Before beginning this activity, look at the drawing of the classroom. You will hear various classroom objects named. Listen and write the letter that corresponds to each item you hear.

1. _____   5. _____

2. _____   6. _____

3. _____   7. _____

4. _____   8. _____

Actividad B ¿Cierto o falso?

Indicate whether the following statements are true (**cierto**) or false (**falso**).

	CIERTO	FALSO
1. La tiza es para (*is for*) la pizarra.	☐	☐
2. La mochila es para la pantalla.	☐	☐
3. El reloj indica la hora (*tells time*).	☐	☐
4. La puerta es para entrar en (*entering*) la sala.	☐	☐
5. El borrador es para la pizarra.	☐	☐
6. Típicamente, en una pantalla hay libros.	☐	☐

Go to page 16 to complete ¡**Acción!** 5.

PRONUNCIACIÓN: r, rr

Paso 1 The pronunciation of the letters **r** and **rr** in Spanish is not at all like the English *r* sound. Spanish has two **r** sounds: the flap and the trill. When the single **r** appears between two vowels, the sound is a flap, similar to the double *tt* or double *dd* in the English words *latter* and *ladder*. The trill sound (a rapidly repeated flap) is used for all other occurrences of single **r** (as the first letter of a word or phrase or following other consonants) and with the double **rr.**

Paso 2 Listen to the following words. Note the difference in the pronunciation of the paired words. Don't worry about the meanings of the words; just focus on their pronunciation.

Teresa	Roberto
pero	perro
para	parra
caro	carro
coro	corro

Paso 3 Listen to and repeat the following words. Try to pronounce the **r** sounds as best as you can.

1. Ramón
2. reloj
3. borrador
4. eres
5. padre (*father*)
6. pizarra
7. Rodrigo
8. literatura
9. nombre
10. carrera

Gramática

Actividad C ¿Dónde está?

Circle the location that corresponds to each landmark.

1. El río Amazonas...
   a. está en Australia.
   b. está en Sudamérica.
   c. está en Asia.

2. Los Pirineos...
   a. están en Europa.
   b. están en Centroamérica.
   c. están en Asia.

3. La Estatua de la Libertad...
   a. está en Egipto.
   b. está en Nueva York.
   c. está en París.

4. Las ruinas mayas...
   a. están en Europa.
   b. están en Centroamérica.
   c. están en Asia.

5. La Torre Eiffel...
   a. está en París.
   b. está en Nueva York.
   c. está en Madrid.

6. La Esfinge (*Sphinx*)...
   a. está en España.
   b. está en Francia.
   c. está en Egipto.

7. El Puente Golden Gate...
   a. está en Chicago.
   b. está en San Francisco.
   c. está en San Diego.

8. El Canal de Panamá...
   a. está en Centroamérica.
   b. está en Sudamérica.
   c. está en Norteamérica.

Actividad D   ¿A quién se refiere? (*To whom does it refer?*)

Listen to each statement and write the letter of the person(s) to whom it refers. Each statement will be read twice.

1. _____
2. _____
3. _____
4. _____
5. _____
6. _____

   a. yo (*the speaker*)
   b. mis (*my*) compañeros y yo
   c. mis amigos
   d. la profesora
   e. tú (*the listener*)
   f. tú y tus (*your*) compañeros (*in Spain*)

> Go to page 16 to complete **¡Acción! 6.**

PRONUNCIACIÓN: h, j, gi/ge, gue, gui

Paso 1   In Spanish, the letter **h** is always silent and never pronounced like its English counterpart.* However, the letters **j** (and occasionally **x**), as well as the sequences **gi** and **ge**, are pronounced similar to the English *h* but a bit further back in the throat. Listen to the pronunciation of the following words. Don't worry about the meanings of the words; just focus on their pronunciation.

hora	hermano	hola	alcohol
jirafa	pasaje		
México	Oaxaca		
geología	gerente		

Paso 2   Note that when **g** is followed by **u,** it is pronounced similar to the English *g* in *get.* However, the **u** is not pronounced before **e** or **i.**

guerra	guía	águila
guardo	agua	

Paso 3   For words where the **u** is pronounced between **g** and **e** or **i,** the *umlaut* (double dots) is added above the **u: ü.**

   bilingüe   lingüístico

Paso 4   Listen to and repeat the following words. Try to pronounce the boldfaced consonants as best as you can. Again, don't worry about the meanings of the words; just focus on their pronunciation.

1. hí**g**ado
2. **h**onesto
3. ho**j**a
4. **g**i**g**ante
5. **g**iro
6. **g**ente
7. **g**uión
8. **g**uitarra
9. **g**uerra
10. **j**ugar
11. **g**ringo
12. **g**eografía

_____

*In Spanish, **h** does combine with **c** to make the **ch** sound, similar to the English *ch* in *church;* for example, **China** and **mochila.**

 # ¡Acción!*

¡Acción! 1   ¿Cómo se llama... ?

Complete the exchange with appropriate statements in Spanish and information that is true for you. Use complete sentences when possible.

—Hola. Soy Enrique. ¿Cómo te llamas?

1. _____

—Mucho gusto.

2. _____

—¿Cuál es tu apellido?

3. _____

—Gracias por la información.

¡Acción! 2   ¿De dónde son?

Write sentences to describe the origin of each person. You may state a city, state, or a country.

1. tú _____

2. Arnold Schwarzenegger _____

3. Nicole Kidman y Russell Crowe _____

¡Acción! 3   Mis (My) clases

Write the name of the subject you would take to study the following topics.

1. el comportamiento (behavior) humano: _____

2. el estudio de los organismos vivos (living): _____

3. la programación y lenguaje (language) de las computadoras: _____

4. la Revolución mexicana: _____

5. las operaciones de compañías como (like) Sears, Citibank o McDonald's: _____

*The ¡Acción! activities are designed to be completed as you finish the corresponding sections in the lesson. There are no answers in the Answer Key for these activities. When you have completed all of the ¡Acción! activities for this lesson, you should tear them out of the *Manual* and hand them in to your instructor.

¡Acción! 4 ¿Qué hay?

Make a list of things that there are in your study or bedroom and in your classroom. Include the definite or indefinite articles in your lists. Compare the lists and circle the items they have in common.

EN MI CUARTO (*ROOM*) HAY...   EN LA SALA DE CLASE HAY...

_____   _____

_____   _____

_____   _____

_____   _____

_____   _____

¡Acción! 5 En la universidad

List five of the buildings on your campus. In Spanish, the name given to a building follows the type of building it is. For example, Pennington Library would be **la Biblioteca Pennington.** After completing your list, check the buildings you take classes in or visit on a regular basis.

1. _____ ☐

2. _____ ☐

3. _____ ☐

4. _____ ☐

5. _____ ☐

¡Acción! 6 Lugares (*Places*) famosos

Write complete sentences to name five famous cities and the countries where they are located. Use the verb **estar.**

1. _____

2. _____

3. _____

4. _____

5. _____

Sobre los horarios

OBJETIVOS

IN THIS LESSON, YOU WILL CONTINUE TO PRACTICE:

- numbers 0–30
- regular -ar verbs to talk about daily schedules
- days of the week
- expressing the need or desire to do something
- talking about time
- possessive adjectives

Vocabulario

Llevo 15 créditos. **Numbers 0–30** ✱

Actividad A La guía telefónica (*phone book*)

▲ You will hear a series of telephone numbers. Listen and write down what you hear. Use numerals in your responses; do not spell out the numbers. You will hear each telephone number twice.

1. _____–_____   5. _____–_____

2. _____–_____   6. _____–_____

3. _____–_____   7. _____–_____

4. _____–_____   8. _____–_____

Actividad B ¿Cuántos son?

▲ You will hear a series of math problems. Write the problem and the correct answer. Use numerals in your responses; do not spell out the numbers. You will hear each problem twice.

VOCABULARIO ÚTIL

más	plus
menos	minus
son	equals

1. _____   5. _____

2. _____   6. _____

3. _____   7. _____

4. _____   8. _____

Actividad C ¿Cierto o falso?

Indicate whether each of the following statements is true (**cierto**) or false (**falso**).

		CIERTO	FALSO
1.	Treinta menos seis son veinticinco.	☐	☐
2.	Seis más once son diecisiete.	☐	☐
3.	Catorce menos uno son tres.	☐	☐
4.	Diez más veinte son treinta.	☐	☐

		CIERTO	FALSO
5.	Nueve más doce son once.	☐	☐
6.	Dos más trece son cinco.	☐	☐
7.	Doce menos uno son once.	☐	☐
8.	Tres más dos son quince.	☐	☐

 Go to page 29 to complete ¡Acción! 1.

Gramática

Estudio y trabajo.

 Regular -ar Verbs

Actividad D **¿A quién se refiere?** (**To whom does it refer?**)

Listen to each statement and write the letter of the person(s) to whom it refers. Pay attention to the verb endings. You will hear each statement twice.

1. _____
2. _____
3. _____
4. _____
5. _____
6. _____

a. yo (*the speaker*)
b. tú (*the listener*)
c. el estudiante típico
d. mis (*my*) compañeros y yo
e. tú y tus (*your*) compañeros (*in Spain*)
f. los estudiantes típicos

Actividad E **¿Quién es?**

Match the statements with the person(s) they describe.

1. _____ Canta en español.
2. _____ Cantan en español.
3. _____ Practican el tenis.
4. _____ Practica el tenis.
5. _____ Estudiamos español.
6. _____ Estudian español.
7. _____ Mira películas.
8. _____ Miro películas.

a. Venus y Serena Williams
b. yo
c. Mark Anthony y Enrique Iglesias
d. mis compañeros de clase
e. Roger Federer
f. Ricky Martin
g. Roger Ebert
h. mis compañeros de clase y yo

 Go to page 29 to complete ¡Acción! 2.

Vocabulario

Los días de la semana   **Days of the week**

Actividad A El horario de Elena

First, take some time to study Elena's class schedule. Then listen to the statements about her schedule. Indicate whether each statement you hear is true (**cierto**) or false (**falso**). You will hear each statement twice.

	LUNES	MARTES	MIÉRCOLES	JUEVES	VIERNES	SÁBADO	DOMINGO
8:00	química	química (laboratorio)	química		química	trabajo	
9:00	biología	biología (laboratorio)	biología	economía (hasta las 10:15)	biología	trabajo	
10:00	literatura		literatura	—	literatura	trabajo	
11:00	francés	francés (laboratorio)	francés		francés	trabajo	
12:00							
1:00	trabajo	trabajo	trabajo	trabajo			
2:00	trabajo	trabajo	trabajo	trabajo			
3:00	trabajo	trabajo	trabajo	trabajo			

	CIERTO	FALSO
1.	☐	☐
2.	☐	☐
3.	☐	☐
4.	☐	☐
5.	☐	☐
6.	☐	☐
7.	☐	☐
8.	☐	☐

Actividad B ¿Qué día es hoy?

Circle the response that most logically completes the statement.

1. Si hoy es lunes, mañana (*tomorrow*) es...

    a. domingo.
    b. martes.
    c. jueves.

2. Los días del fin de semana son...

    a. sábado y domingo.
    b. martes y jueves.
    c. jueves y viernes.

3. El Día de Acción de Gracias (*Thanksgiving*) siempre (*always*) es un...

    a. jueves.
    b. domingo.
    c. miércoles.

4. Los católicos y muchos otros (*many other*) cristianos van a la iglesia (*go to church*) el...

    a. lunes.
    b. sábado.
    c. domingo.

5. El día antes del (*before*) jueves es el...

    a. lunes.
    b. miércoles.
    c. martes.

6. El primer (*first*) día de la semana es...

    a. sábado.
    b. lunes.
    c. jueves.

Actividad C El horario de Claudia

Listen to Claudia describe her schedule. Then indicate if the following statements are true (**cierto**) or false (**falso**), based on what you hear. Feel free to listen to the description more than once if you like.

		CIERTO	FALSO
1.	Claudia tiene clases o laboratorio todos los días de la semana.	☐	☐
2.	Tiene una clase de biología los jueves.	☐	☐
3.	Tiene dos laboratorios los martes.	☐	☐
4.	Tiene las mismas (*same*) clases los lunes y viernes.	☐	☐
5.	Estudia los sábados y domingos.	☐	☐
6.	No trabaja los miércoles.	☐	☐

 Go to page 30 to complete **¡Acción! 3.**

Gramática

Necesito estudiar. **Verb + *infinitive***

 Actividad D   ¿A quién se refiere?

Listen to each statement and write the letter of the person(s) to whom it refers. Pay attention to the verb endings. You will hear each statement twice.

1. _____
2. _____
3. _____
4. _____
5. _____
6. _____

a. yo (*the speaker*)
b. los estudiantes de español
c. tú y tus amigos (*in Spain*)
d. tú (*the listener*)
e. el profesor
f. mis amigos y yo

Actividad E   ¿Qué necesitan hacer?

Match each statement with the most logical situation.

1. _____ Estás muy cansado/a (*tired*).

2. _____ Hay un examen en dos días y tu amigo no está preparado.

3. _____ Tengo muchas distracciones.

4. _____ Tus amigos desean investigar un tópico.

5. _____ No dedicáis suficiente tiempo a vuestra (*your*) familia.

6. _____ No estudias lo suficiente (*enough*).

7. _____ Tu amigo desea visitar Guanajuato.

8. _____ No tengo el libro.

a. Necesitáis pasar más tiempo con ellos.
b. Necesito concentrarme (*to concentrate*).
c. Necesita estudiar.
d. Necesitas descansar.
e. Necesitan navegar la red.
f. Necesito comprar uno.
g. Necesitas memorizar el vocabulario.
h. Necesita viajar a México.

Actividad F ¿Qué necesitas?

Circle the response that most logically completes each sentence.

1. Estudiáis piano.

   Necesitáis…
   a. jugar.
   b. empezar.
   c. practicar.

2. Hay un examen mañana y no estoy preparada.

   Necesito…
   a. regresar a casa.
   b. hablar por teléfono.
   c. estudiar.

3. Tu amigo vive (*lives*) en un apartamento.

   Necesita…
   a. hablar con amigos.
   b. preparar la composición.
   c. pagar el alquiler.

4. Deseas información sobre Quito, Ecuador.

   Necesitas…
   a. navegar la red.
   b. practicar tenis.
   c. tomar una cerveza.

5. Los miembros de la clase estudian muchas horas.

   Necesitan…
   a. tomar café.
   b. pagar las cuentas.
   c. tocar la guitarra.

6. Deseas estudiar música.

   Necesitas…
   a. visitar a la familia.
   b. tomar una clase.
   c. charlar con el profesor.

7. Uds. escuchan al profesor de historia mientras explica (*while he explains*) mucha información importante.

   Necesitan…
   a. tomar apuntes.
   b. descansar en clase.
   c. practicar.

8. Deseamos descansar después de (*after*) trabajar todo el día.

   Necesitamos…
   a. practicar un deporte.
   b. regresar a casa.
   c. tomar apuntes.

 Go to page 30 to complete ¡Acción! 4.

Vocabulario

¿A qué hora?

Telling Time

 Actividad A ¿Qué hora es?

You will hear a series of time statements. Listen and match each statement to the corresponding clock. You will hear each statement twice.

1. ____   a. `12:10`

2. ____   b. `03:15`

3. ____

4. ____   c. `08:20`

5. ____

6. ____   d. `07:05`

7. ____   e. `04:35`

8. ____

　　　　　f. `09:45`

　　　　　g. `01:25`

　　　　　h. `10:30`

Actividad B ¿A qué hora?

Circle the response that reflects the time mentioned in each statement.

1. El baile (*dance*) es a las diez.   **a.** 2:00   **b.** 10:00

2. La clase termina (*ends*) a la una menos diez.   **a.** 12:50   **b.** 1:10

3. La conferencia (*meeting*) es a las tres y cuarto.   **a.** 3:04   **b.** 3:15

4. La fiesta (*party*) es a las siete y media.   **a.** 6:30   **b.** 7:30

5. La clase es a las once menos cuarto.   **a.** 10:45   **b.** 11:15

6. El concierto es a mediodía.   **a.** 12:00 A.M.   **b.** 12:00 P.M.

7. El trabajo comienza (*begins*) a las nueve menos cuarto. **a.** 8:45   **b.** 8:56

8. La película termina a las cinco.   **a.** 5:00   **b.** 6:00

Actividad C ¿Cuándo?

Circle the correct response to complete each of the following statements.

1. Son las siete. La fiesta es a las nueve. La fiesta es en…
    a. tres horas.   **b.** dos horas.   **c.** cuatro horas.

2. Son las diez. La clase es en cuatro horas. La clase es a las…
    a. dos.   **b.** tres.   **c.** seis.

3. El concierto es a las ocho. El concierto es en una hora. Son las…
    a. cinco.   **b.** seis.   **c.** siete.

4. Son las seis. Trabajo a las nueve. Trabajo en…
    a. dos horas.   **b.** tres horas.   **c.** cuatro horas.

5. Son las dos. El trabajo termina en cuatro horas. El trabajo termina a las…
    a. cinco.   **b.** seis.   **c.** siete.

6. La conferencia es a las tres. La conferencia es en una hora. Son las…
    a. dos.   **b.** tres.   **c.** cuatro.

  Go to page 31 to complete ¡**Acción!** 5.

Gramática

Es mi libro.   **Unstressed Possessive Adjectives**

Actividad D ¿Qué tienen (*do they have*)?

Circle the word that best completes each statement.

1. Los autos son de mi padre (*father*).

   _____ autos son grandes (*big*).
   a. Su
   b. Sus
   c. Tus

2. Necesitáis hacer la tarea (*to do homework*).

   _____ tarea es importante.
   a. Vuestros
   b. Vuestra
   c. Vuestras

3. Tienes muchos amigos.

   _____ mejor (*best*) amigo se llama Raúl, ¿verdad? (*right?*)
   a. Tu
   b. Su
   c. Sus

4. Soy estudiante de idiomas.

   _____ profesor de portugués es del Brasil.
   a. Su
   b. Mis
   c. Mi

5. El escritorio es de Alberto y Paco.

   _____ escritorio es viejo (*old*).
   a. Su
   b. Sus
   c. Vuestro

6. Necesitamos comprar los libros.

   _____ libro de biología es muy caro (*expensive*).
   a. Vuestro
   b. Nuestros
   c. Nuestro

Actividad E ¿De quién es?

Listen to each statement and write the letter of the person(s) to whom the possessive adjective refers. You will hear each statement twice.

1. ____
2. ____
3. ____
4. ____
5. ____
6. ____
7. ____
8. ____

a. la persona que habla (yo)
b. la persona que escucha (tú)
c. un amigo
d. nosotros
e. vosotros

Go to page 31 to complete ¡Acción! 6.

¡A escuchar!*

Antes de escuchar (*Before listening*)

Paso 1 In a moment you will listen to two people, Roberto and Marisela, talking about the first episode of *Sol y viento*. What do you think they will do? (You will verify your answer after listening.)

☐ They will summarize what happened.

☐ They will offer opinions about what happened.

☐ They will talk about whether they liked the episode or not.

Paso 2 Here are some new words and phrases you will encounter. Study them before listening.

ganarse la vida	to earn a living
quizás	perhaps

A escuchar

Now listen to the conversation.

> **Estrategia**
> You will hear several new words that are not in the prior list. They are cognates (words that look alike in two or more languages). Listen for them and try to understand them in context.

(continued)

---

*¡A... *Let's listen!*

▲ Después de escuchar (*After listening*)

Paso 1 Verify your answer to **Paso 1** of **Antes de escuchar.** Do Roberto and Marisela

☐ summarize what happened?

☐ offer opinions about what happened?

☐ talk about whether they liked the episode or not?

Paso 2 Answer the following questions based on what you heard.

1. Roberto tiene una opinión favorable de Mario.

☐ sí

☐ no

2. Marisela no está de acuerdo (*doesn't agree*) con Roberto.

☐ sí

☐ no

3. ¿Qué opina Marisela de Carlos, el personaje de *Sol y viento*?

☐ Cree que (*She thinks that*) tiene un secreto.

☐ Cree que es muy servil.

☐ Le gusta mucho.

Paso 3 Listen to the exchange between Roberto and Marisela again. Use the strategy of listening for cognates in context by listing the cognates you hear for the English words in the list.

expression　　*possibly*　　*preoccupation*　　*servile*　　*sinister*

1. _____

2. _____

3. _____

4. _____

5. _____

Paso 4 In the following space, write two to three sentences about whether you agree with Roberto or with Marisela about the character Mario.

VOCABULARIO ÚTIL

creo que...	I think that . . .
(No) Estoy de acuerdo.	I (don't) agree.
porque	because
(No) Tiene razón.	He/She is right (wrong).

_____

_____

_____

_____

 **¡Acción!***

¡Acción! 1 ¿Cuántos créditos?

Spell out each number correctly in Spanish.

1. 15 _____

2. 13 _____

3. 21 _____

4. 10 _____

5. 11 _____

6. 19 _____

¡Acción! 2 ¿Con qué frecuencia?

Name three things you do every day (**cada día**), two things you do every week (**cada semana**), and one thing you do every month (**cada mes**).

CADA DÍA

1. _____

2. _____

3. _____

CADA SEMANA

4. _____

5. _____

CADA MES

6. _____

_____

*Remember that the **¡Acción!** activities are designed to be completed as you finish the corresponding sections in the lesson. There are no answers in the Answer Key for these activities. When you have completed all of the **¡Acción!** activities for this lesson, you should tear them out of the *Manual* and turn them in to your instructor.

¡Acción! 3 Tus clases

Write a paragraph of twenty-five to fifty words about your class schedule. Be sure to answer the following questions.

How many classes are you taking?

How many credits are you taking?

How many classes do you have on each day of the week?

_____

_____

_____

_____

_____

_____

_____

¡Acción! 4 Deseos (*Wishes*) y obligaciones

Write sentences listing three things that you want to do but can't. Then write sentences listing three things you need to do but would rather not. Use **desear** + *infinitive* in the first group of sentences and **necesitar** + *infinitive* in the second.

LO QUE (*WHAT*) DESEO HACER (*TO DO*)

1. _____

_____

2. _____

_____

3. _____

_____

LO QUE NECESITO HACER

1. _____

_____

2. _____

_____

3. _____

_____

¡Acción! 5 Mi horario

List all of your classes and the time of day they meet. Spell out the times in Spanish. (Don't use numerals.)

MODELO: Tengo la clase de ____ a la(s) ____ de la ____.

1. _____
2. _____
3. _____
4. _____
5. _____
6. _____
7. _____

¡Acción! 6 Algunas cosas favoritas (*Some favorite things*)

Using the correct possessive adjectives, write a sentence about each item for each person.

YO

1. clases favoritas: _____

2. la clase más difícil (*the most difficult class*): _____

MIS COMPAÑEROS DE CLASE Y YO

3. el libro de español: _____

UN AMIGO (UNA AMIGA) _____ (NOMBRE)

4. clases favoritas: _____

5. la clase más difícil: _____

Más sobre las actividades

OBJETIVOS

IN THIS LESSON, YOU WILL CONTINUE TO PRACTICE:

- **interrogative (question) words**

- **regular -er and -ir verbs to talk about activities**

- **talking about months, seasons, and weather**

- **expressing immediate and planned future events with ir**

- **describing people using adjectives**

- **adjective agreement**

Vocabulario

¿Cuándo?   **Summary of Interrogative Words**

 Actividad A   Unas preguntas (*questions*)

First, read the following questions. Then listen to each response and write the letter of the most logical question in the blank.

1. _____
2. _____
3. _____
4. _____
5. _____
6. _____
7. _____
8. _____

a. ¿Cuándo es tu clase de historia?
b. ¿Con quién hablas?
c. ¿Cuántas sillas hay en la clase?
d. ¿De dónde eres?
e. ¿Cuál es tu clase favorita?
f. ¿Cómo te llamas?
g. ¿Adónde viajas este fin de semana?
h. ¿Qué estudias?

Actividad B   Respuestas (*Answers*) lógicas

Indicate the most logical response to each of the following questions.

1. ¿Quiénes están en la clase?

   ☐ los escritorios

   ☐ unas chicas

2. ¿Cuál es tu clase favorita?

   ☐ la informática

   ☐ el auditorio

3. ¿Dónde estudias, por lo general?

   ☐ en la librería

   ☐ en la biblioteca

4. ¿Cuándo es la clase de química?

   ☐ los lunes y miércoles

   ☐ los sábados y domingos

5. ¿A quién llamas?

   ☐ mi mochila

   ☐ a mi amigo

6. ¿Dónde están los escritorios?

   ☐ en el gimnasio

   ☐ en la sala de clase

7. ¿Qué es *Como agua para chocolate*?

   ☐ una película mexicana

   ☐ una clase de sociología

8. ¿Por qué estás en la librería?

   ☐ Necesito comprar un libro.

   ☐ Necesito estudiar.

Actividad C Una entrevista

The question words from this interview with a famous Spanish actor are missing. Write the letter of the correct interrogative word to complete each question.

—¿_____¹ se llama?

—Me llamo Antonio.

—¿_____² es su apellido?

—Es Banderas.

—Muy bien, señor Banderas. ¿_____³ es Ud.?

—Originalmente, soy de España, pero ahora vivoª en los Estados Unidos con mi familia.

—¿_____⁴ es su esposa?ᵇ

—Melanie Griffith.

—¿_____⁵ hijosᶜ tienen Uds.?

—Tenemos tres hijos, en total.

—Ud. es actor en muchas películas. ¿_____⁶ va a hacerᵈ otra película?

—Muy pronto.ᵉ

a. Cómo
b. Cuál
c. Cuándo
d. Cuántos
e. De dónde
f. Quién

ªahora... *now I live* ᵇ*wife* ᶜ*children* ᵈva... *are you going to make* ᵉMuy... *Very soon.*

  Go to page 45 to complete ¡**Acción! 1.**

Gramática

¿Dónde vives?

Actividad D ¿A quién se refiere?

Listen to each statement and write the letter of the person(s) to whom it refers. Pay attention to the verb endings. You will hear each statement twice.

1. _____
2. _____
3. _____
4. _____
5. _____
6. _____

a. yo (*the speaker*)
b. tú (*the listener*)
c. la profesora
d. mis compañeros y yo
e. tú y tus compañeros (*in Spain*)
f. los estudiantes

Actividad E ¿Qué hace (*does he/she do*)?

Match each verb with a sentence fragment to form logical statements about your instructor. Next time you are in class, ask your instructor how often he or she does each activity.

1. _____ Bebe…
2. _____ Abre…
3. _____ Asiste…
4. _____ Escribe…
5. _____ Corre…
6. _____ Recibe…
7. _____ Come…
8. _____ Aprende…

a. una carta (*letter*) a un amigo.
b. en un restaurante.
c. cerveza.
d. algo nuevo.
e. el libro de texto.
f. a un concierto de música clásica.
g. a clase para no llegar tarde.
h. correo electrónico de los estudiantes.

 Go to page 45 to complete **¡Acción! 2.**

SEGUNDA PARTE

Vocabulario

¡Hace calor en junio! **Months, Weather, and Seasons**

 Actividad A ¿Qué haces (*do you do*)?

Listen to each weather statement and circle the letter of the most logical activity. You will hear each statement twice.

1. **a.** comer en casa

    b. comer en el patio

2. **a.** tomar café

    b. beber una cerveza fría

3. **a.** cerrar (*to close*) las ventanas

    b. abrir las ventanas

4. **a.** tomar el sol

    b. leer una novela

5. **a.** hacer (*to have*) un picnic

    b. ver un vídeo

6. **a.** viajar en auto

    b. descansar en casa

7. **a.** navegar en barco de vela (*to sail*)

    b. navegar en la red

8. **a.** correr en el parque

    b. tomar el sol

 Actividad B Los meses

Listen to the name of each month. Circle the letter of the number that corresponds to that month. **Note:** 01 = January, 12 = December.

1. **a.** 02   **b.** 03   **c.** 04

2. **a.** 10   **b.** 11   **c.** 12

3. **a.** 06   **b.** 04   **c.** 01

4. **a.** 09   **b.** 04   **c.** 07

5. **a.** 05   **b.** 08   **c.** 11

6. **a.** 02   **b.** 05   **c.** 09

7. **a.** 10   **b.** 11   **c.** 12

8. **a.** 06   **b.** 07   **c.** 08

Actividad C Las estaciones

Paso 1 Read each statement and indicate whether it describes weather in the Northern (N) or Southern (S) Hemisphere.

		N	S				N	S
1.	Hace frío en julio.	☐	☐	**5.**	Hace calor en agosto.		☐	☐
2.	Nieva en diciembre.	☐	☐	**6.**	Nieva en junio.		☐	☐
3.	Hace frío en enero.	☐	☐	**7.**	Hace frío en febrero.		☐	☐
4.	Hace calor en diciembre.	☐	☐	**8.**	Hace calor en enero.		☐	☐

Paso 2 Now indicate the season being described.

		VERANO	INVIERNO
1.	Hace frío en julio.	☐	☐
2.	Nieva en diciembre.	☐	☐
3.	Hace frío en enero.	☐	☐
4.	Hace calor en diciembre.	☐	☐
5.	Hace calor en agosto.	☐	☐
6.	Nieva en junio.	☐	☐
7.	Hace frío en febrero.	☐	☐
8.	Hace calor en enero.	☐	☐

 Go to page 45 to complete **¡Acción! 3.**

Gramática

¿Vas a estudiar esta noche?

Ir + a + *infinitive*

 Actividad D **¿Qué van a hacer (*to do*)?**

Listen to each question and write the letter of the most logical response.

1. _____

2. _____

3. _____

4. _____

5. _____

6. _____

a. Sí, tengo un examen mañana.
b. Sí, voy a ver París.
c. No, va a viajar todo el verano.
d. Sí, vamos al cine (*movies*) a las tres.
e. No, vamos a visitar Italia.
f. Sí, tenemos un examen mañana.

Actividad E ¿Qué vas a hacer?

Match each situation with the most logical response. When you finish, mark when you will most likely do the activity.

1. _____ Tú y tu amigo tienen un examen mañana.

☐ dentro de poco   ☐ la semana entrante

☐ mañana   ☐ el próximo verano

☐ pasado mañana   ☐ en un año

☐ en unos cuantos días

2. _____ Necesitas el libro de texto para la clase de química.

☐ dentro de poco   ☐ la semana entrante

☐ mañana   ☐ el próximo verano

☐ pasado mañana   ☐ en un año

☐ en unos cuantos días

3. _____ Deseas visitar el Perú, Chile y el Ecuador.

☐ dentro de poco   ☐ la semana entrante

☐ mañana   ☐ el próximo verano

☐ pasado mañana   ☐ en un año

☐ en unos cuantos días

4. _____ Hay un programa muy interesante en el canal 16.

☐ dentro de poco   ☐ la semana entrante

☐ mañana   ☐ el próximo verano

☐ pasado mañana   ☐ en un año

☐ en unos cuantos días

5. _____ Necesitas información sobre los animales de Costa Rica.

☐ dentro de poco   ☐ la semana entrante

☐ mañana   ☐ el próximo verano

☐ pasado mañana   ☐ en un año

☐ en unos cuantos días

6. _____ Hace muy buen tiempo y deseas tomar el sol.

☐ dentro de poco   ☐ la semana entrante

☐ mañana   ☐ el próximo verano

☐ pasado mañana   ☐ en un año

☐ en unos cuantos días

¿QUÉ VAS A HACER?

a. Voy a navegar la red.
b. Voy a ir a la librería.
c. Voy a ver la televisión.
d. Voy a estudiar con mi amigo.
e. Voy a invitar a mis amigos a la playa (*beach*).
f. Voy a viajar a Sudamérica.

 Go to page 46 to complete ¡**Acción!** 4.

Vocabulario

Es un hombre serio.

 Adjectives

 Actividad A ¿A quién se refiere?

First, read the following sentences. Then listen to each description and write the letter of the sentence that best corresponds with it. You will hear each description twice.

1. _____
2. _____
3. _____
4. _____
5. _____
6. _____
7. _____
8. _____

   a. Prefiere (*He prefers*) el partido (*party*) republicano.
   b. Tiene una idea exagerada de su propia (*own*) importancia.
   c. Habla mucho.
   d. No guarda (*keep*) secretos.
   e. Pierde (*He loses*) la paciencia fácilmente (*easily*).
   f. Es fascinante.
   g. Piensa mucho en (*He thinks a lot about*) la filosofía y las teorías.
   h. Cree que todo va mal.

Actividad B Sinónimos

Match each adjective in column A with its synonym or related word in column B.

A	B
1. _____ agradable	**a.** estimulante
2. _____ indiscreto	**b.** organizado
3. _____ sospechoso	**c.** chismoso
4. _____ interesante	**d.** reservado
5. _____ metódico	**e.** simpático
6. _____ introvertido	**f.** desconfiado

Actividad C Antónimos

Match the adjective in column A to its opposite in column B.

	A		B
1.	_____ malicioso	**a.**	apasionado
2.	_____ indiferente	**b.**	optimista
		c.	simpático
3.	_____ aburrido	**d.**	caótico
4.	_____ pesimista	**e.**	humilde
		f.	ingenuo
5.	_____ sabio	**g.**	interesante
6.	_____ listo	**h.**	tonto
7.	_____ arrogante		
8.	_____ metódico		

 Go to page 46 to complete **¡Acción! 5.**

Gramática

 Es una mujer seria.   **Adjective Placement and Agreement**

Actividad D ¿A quién se refiere?

Listen to each adjective and circle the person(s) to whom it refers. Pay attention to adjective endings. If the adjective refers to both people, circle **los dos.**

1. _____	**a.** David Letterman	**b.** Ellen DeGeneres	**c.** los dos
2. _____	**a.** Laura Bush	**b.** Rush Limbaugh	**c.** los dos
3. _____	**a.** Madame Curie	**b.** Albert Einstein	**c.** los dos
4. _____	**a.** Hillary Clinton	**b.** Barack Obama	**c.** los dos
5. _____	**a.** Angelina Jolie	**b.** Brad Pitt	**c.** los dos
6. _____	**a.** Madonna	**b.** Will Smith	**c.** los dos
7. _____	**a.** J.K. Rowling	**b.** Will Ferrell	**c.** los dos
8. _____	**a.** Charles Darwin	**b.** Barbara Walters	**c.** los dos

Actividad E Personas famosas

Circle the correct form of the adjective to complete each sentence. Then indicate whether or not you agree with the statement.

			SÍ	NO
1.	Bill Clinton es…			
	a. sabio.	**b.** sabia.	☐	☐
2.	Las hermanas Williams son…			
	a. ambiciosos.	**b.** ambiciosas.	☐	☐
3.	Rosie O'Donnell es…			
	a. humilde.	**b.** humildes.	☐	☐
4.	Arnold Schwarzenegger es…			
	a. conservador.	**b.** conservadora.	☐	☐
5.	Joan Rivers es…			
	a. chismoso.	**b.** chismosa.	☐	☐
6.	Oprah Winfrey es…			
	a. trabajador.	**b.** trabajadora.	☐	☐
7.	Charlie Chaplin es…			
	a. cerebral.	**b.** cerebrales.	☐	☐
8.	Steven Spielberg es…			
	a. imaginativo.	**b.** imaginativa.	☐	☐

 Go to page 46 to complete **¡Acción! 6.**

 # Para escribir

Antes de escribir

For this activity, you will write descriptions of Jaime and Mario, comparing and contrasting them. From the list of adjectives below, indicate which ones best describe either character (or both). Share your ideas with someone else.

	ADJETIVOS	JAIME	MARIO
1.	guapo (*handsome*)	☐	☐
2.	ambicioso	☐	☐
3.	simpático	☐	☐
4.	joven (*young*)	☐	☐
5.	inteligente	☐	☐
6.	trabajador	☐	☐

ADJETIVOS	JAIME	MARIO
7. bilingüe	☐	☐
8. serio	☐	☐
9. gregario	☐	☐
10. reservado	☐	☐

A escribir

Paso 1   Now that you have made some preliminary decisions about the personalities of these two characters, you must decide how you will organize your thoughts. Select one of the possibilities below.

☐ write about Jaime first, then Mario

☐ write about Mario first, then Jaime

☐ use the personality traits to compare and contrast each person as you go

Paso 2   Now draft your description on a separate sheet of paper. The following phrases may be helpful in writing your descriptions.

al contrario	on the other hand
en cambio	on the other hand
igualmente	equally
no tanto	not as much
pero	but
sin embargo	however
también	also
y	and

Paso 3   Exchange compositions with a classmate so that you can provide initial feedback for each other. As you read each other's composition, check for the following things.

☐ overall sense, meaning

☐ adjective/noun agreement

☐ subject/verb agreement

☐ spelling

Al entregar la composición

Paso 1   Review the feedback you received from your classmate. As you go through your composition, remember to check for the following:

☐ adjective/noun agreement

☐ subject/verb agreement

Paso 2   Now finalize your composition and turn it in to your instructor.

🎬 ¡Acción!

¡Acción! 1 ¿Y tú?

Answer each of the following questions in Spanish using complete sentences.

1. ¿Cómo te llamas?

_____

2. ¿Cuál es tu clase favorita?

_____

3. ¿De dónde eres?

_____

4. ¿Dónde vives?

_____

5. ¿Cuántas personas hay en tu clase de español?

_____

¡Acción! 2 Preguntas para un compañero (una compañera) de clase

Write five questions for a classmate using any of the following verbs.

abrir	beber	correr	recibir
aprender	comer	escribir	ver
asistir	comprender	leer	vivir

1. _____

2. _____

3. _____

4. _____

5. _____

¡Acción! 3 Los meses y el tiempo

For each month listed, write in which season it occurs and what the weather is normally like at your university.

MODELO: septiembre: *otoño. No hace mucho calor y no hace frío.*

1. marzo: _____

2. julio: _____

3. octubre: _____

4. diciembre: _____

¡Acción! 4 ¿Qué vamos a hacer?

Write five sentences about what you and your friends or family are going to do this weekend using the **nosotros** form of **ir + a.**

1. _____
2. _____
3. _____
4. _____
5. _____

¡Acción! 5 Un amigo mío (*of mine*)

Write three or four sentences describing a male friend. Use the adjectives you have learned in this section and look up others in the dictionary, if necessary.

_____

_____

_____

_____

¡Acción! 6 ¿Cómo son?

Choose one male and one female celebrity or politician. Write a twenty-five to fifty-word paragraph, comparing and contrasting them. Use as many adjectives as you can.

_____

_____

_____

_____

_____

_____

_____

En la universidad y la ciudad

IN THIS LESSON, YOU WILL CONTINUE TO PRACTICE:

- **numbers 31–100 and expressing age**

- **talking about activities using verbs that end in -go**

- **prepositions of location to express where things and places are**

- **expressing where places are and what is happening right now using the verb estar**

- **names of places in the city**

- **talking about activities using stem-changing verbs**

Vocabulario

¿Cuántos años tiene?   **Numbers 31–100**

Actividad A ¿Qué número es?

▲ You will hear a series of numbers in Spanish. Write down the numerals that you hear.

MODELO: (*you hear*) treinta y dos
(*you write*) 32

1. _____

2. _____

3. _____

4. _____

5. _____

6. _____

7. _____

8. _____

Actividad B ¿Quién es mayor (*older*)?

▲ **Paso 1** Listen and write the ages of the following pairs of people. Then write the name of the older person of each pair. You will hear each statement twice.

NOMBRE	EDAD	NOMBRE	EDAD	¿QUIÉN ES MAYOR?
1. Leticia	_____	Nancy	_____	_____
2. Sergio	_____	Marcela	_____	_____
3. Rosa María	_____	Marcos	_____	_____
4. Rodrigo	_____	Leonora	_____	_____
5. Alba	_____	Gabriela	_____	_____
6. Pablo	_____	Andrés	_____	_____

Paso 2 Of all the people listed in **Paso 1,** who is the oldest?

_____ es el/la mayor de todos (*the oldest of all*).

Actividad C Las tres edades (*ages*)

Indicate the age group into which the ages fall.

	ADOLESCENTE	ADULTO	ANCIANO (*ELDERLY*)
1. Tiene treinta años.	☐	☐	☐
2. Tiene dieciséis años.	☐	☐	☐
3. Tiene cuarenta y un años.	☐	☐	☐
4. Tiene noventa y tres años.	☐	☐	☐
5. Tiene trece años.	☐	☐	☐
6. Tiene setenta y ocho años.	☐	☐	☐
7. Tiene veintisiete años.	☐	☐	☐
8. Tiene ochenta y dos años.	☐	☐	☐

 Go to page 59 to complete ¡**Acción!** 1.

Gramática

Vengo de los Estados Unidos.　　　　　　　　**Verbs that End in -go**

Actividad D ¿De dónde vengo?

Listen to each statement about what the speaker has, then write the letter of the place from where he or she is coming. You will hear each statement twice.

1. _____
2. _____
3. _____
4. _____
5. _____
6. _____

a. Vengo de la Facultad de Idiomas.
b. Vengo del edificio de matemáticas.
c. Vengo de clase.
d. Vengo de la cafetería.
e. Vengo del auditorio.
f. Vengo de la biblioteca.

Actividad E ¿Estudiante modelo?

Paso 1 Imagine that a student says the following things. Determine whether each statement describes him as a model student.

		SÍ	NO
1.	Salgo de la clase antes de que suene la campana (*before the bell rings*).	☐	☐
2.	Traigo todos los libros necesarios a clase.	☐	☐
3.	Vengo a clase diez minutos tarde todos los días.	☐	☐
4.	Hago la tarea de otras clases mientras habla el profesor (la profesora).	☐	☐
5.	Tengo hecha (*ready*) la tarea.	☐	☐
6.	Pongo la tarea en la mesa del profesor (de la profesora).	☐	☐

Paso 2 Now indicate which behaviors from **Paso 1** describe you (**Lo hago yo**) or not (**No lo hago yo**), then check the sentence that best applies to your classroom behavior.

	LO HAGO YO.	NO LO HAGO YO.
1.	☐	☐
2.	☐	☐
3.	☐	☐
4.	☐	☐
5.	☐	☐
6.	☐	☐

☐ Tengo que cambiar (*change*), porque no soy estudiante modelo.

☐ No tengo que cambiar, porque soy estudiante modelo.

Actividad F ¿Durante (*During*) la clase o fuera (*outside*) de clase?

Listen to the following statements that a student makes about her and her friends' activities. Indicate if the activities typically take place during class (**durante la clase**) or outside of class (**fuera de clase**).

	DURANTE LA CLASE	FUERA DE CLASE
1.	☐	☐
2.	☐	☐
3.	☐	☐
4.	☐	☐
5.	☐	☐
6.	☐	☐

Go to page 59 to complete ¡**Acción!** 2.

SEGUNDA PARTE

Vocabulario

¿Está lejos o cerca?

Prepositions of Location

 Actividad A **¿Cierto o falso?**

Look at the drawing and listen to the statements. Indicate whether each statement is true (**cierto**) or false (**falso**). You will hear each statement twice.

	CIERTO	FALSO		CIERTO	FALSO
1.	☐	☐	**5.**	☐	☐
2.	☐	☐	**6.**	☐	☐
3.	☐	☐	**7.**	☐	☐
4.	☐	☐	**8.**	☐	☐

Actividad B ¿Una universidad norteamericana o hispana?

Based on the cultural information you learned in the textbook, indicate whether the following descriptions best describe a typical university campus in this country or a university campus in a Spanish-speaking country.

1. Los estudiantes toman todas sus clases en la misma facultad.

   ☐ una universidad norteamericana   ☐ una universidad hispana

2. Los estudiantes viven muy cerca de la universidad y caminan a sus clases.

   ☐ una universidad norteamericana   ☐ una universidad hispana

3. Los estudiantes viven bastante lejos de la universidad y llegan en tren o autobús.

   ☐ una universidad norteamericana   ☐ una universidad hispana

4. Alrededor de la universidad hay residencias estudiantiles.

   ☐ una universidad norteamericana   ☐ una universidad hispana

5. Los estudiantes comen en una cafetería cerca de la residencia estudiantil.

   ☐ una universidad norteamericana   ☐ una universidad hispana

6. Los estudiantes hacen cola (*stand in line*) delante del gimnasio para ver el partido (*game*) de basquetbol de la universidad.

   ☐ una universidad norteamericana   ☐ una universidad hispana

Actividad C En la sala de clase

Indicate if these sentences describe a typical classroom or not.

	SÍ	NO
1. La profesora está detrás de los estudiantes.	☐	☐
2. Los estudiantes se sientan (*sit*) debajo de los escritorios.	☐	☐
3. La profesora escribe en la pizarra.	☐	☐
4. Los estudiantes ponen las mochilas al lado de los escritorios.	☐	☐
5. La pizarra está detrás de la pared.	☐	☐
6. Los estudiantes escriben en el cuaderno (*notebook*) delante de ellos.	☐	☐
7. Los libros están en la pared.	☐	☐
8. Las ventanas están entre los estudiantes y el profesor.	☐	☐

Go to page 60 to complete ¡Acción! 3.

Gramática

¿Dónde están y qué están haciendo?

Two Uses of estar

Actividad D Las ciudades de España

Listen to the geographic descriptions of some cities in Spain and indicate if each statement is true (**cierto**) or false (**falso**), based on the map. You will hear each statement twice.

	CIERTO	FALSO
1.	☐	☐
2.	☐	☐
3.	☐	☐
4.	☐	☐
5.	☐	☐
6.	☐	☐
7.	☐	☐
8.	☐	☐

Actividad E ¿Dónde están y qué están haciendo?

Match the place where the student is with what she is doing there.

La estudiante...

1. _____ está en la biblioteca.

2. _____ está en la cafetería.

3. _____ está en el gimnasio.

4. _____ está en el bar Kelly's.

5. _____ está en su salón (*living room*).

6. _____ está enfrente de su computadora.

a. Está bebiendo algo.
b. Está escribiendo algo.
c. Está haciendo ejercicio.
d. Está viendo la televisión.
e. Está buscando un libro.
f. Está comiendo.

 Go to page 60 to complete **¡Acción! 4.**

TERCERA PARTE

Vocabulario

Tengo que ir al banco.

 Places in the City

Actividad A ¿Adónde vas para... ?

Circle where you go to do each activity.

1. Para (*In order to*) ir de compras (*go shopping*) voy...

   a. a un hotel.   **b.** a un restaurante.   **c.** al centro comercial.

2. Para pasear voy...

   a. al parque.   **b.** al cine.   **c.** a una tienda.

3. Para mandar una carta (*send a letter*) voy...

   a. a la escuela.   **b.** a la iglesia.   **c.** al correo.

4. Para viajar voy...

   a. al mercado.   **b.** a la estación del tren.   **c.** a una farmacia.

5. Para bailar voy...

   a. a una discoteca.   **b.** a un estanco.   **c.** a una farmacia.

6. Para comer voy...

    a. a la catedral.   **b.** al restaurante.   **c.** al almacén.

7. Para dormir (*sleep*) voy...

    a. al cajero automático.   **b.** a la tienda.   **c.** al hotel.

Actividad B   Después de clase

Listen as Teresa describes what she has to do after class today. Then match each activity with the corresponding place, based on what you hear. Don't worry if you don't understand every word. Use the information you do understand to make the matches. Pause the audio to match the activities and places. You can listen to the narration as many times as you like. **¡OJO!** Not all of the places listed will be used.

1. _____ caminar con Lidia

2. _____ charlar con Raúl

3. _____ visitar a Juana

4. _____ ir al trabajo

5. _____ trabajar

6. _____ comer con Enrique

7. _____ salir con amigas

8. _____ tomar café con Sara

a. el restaurante
b. la catedral
c. el centro comercial
d. el hospital
e. la plaza
f. el cine
g. la farmacia
h. el supermercado
i. el banco
j. la parada de autobuses

Actividad C   Recomendaciones

Match each statement with the most logical recommendation.

1. _____ Busco la casa de los padres de Catalina.

2. _____ Voy a Monterrey, una ciudad que queda muy lejos.

3. _____ Tengo que comprar medicina para Federico.

4. _____ Deseo hablar con los administradores de la ciudad.

5. _____ Voy a enseñar una clase de niños.

6. _____ Deseo confesarme con (*to confess to*) el cura (*priest*).

7. _____ Deseo ver una película.

8. _____ Tengo que comprar estampillas (*stamps*).

a. Debes ir a la catedral San José.
b. Necesitas ir al cine Estrellísimo.
c. Debes ir al correo central.
d. Debes ir a la farmacia Gutiérrez.
e. Necesitas ir al barrio Jardines.
f. Necesitas ir a la escuela Palomas.
g. Debes ir a la estación Mercedes.
h. Tienes que ir al ayuntamiento del centro.

 Go to page 61 to complete **¡Acción! 5.**

Gramática

Puedo caminar. $\qquad$ **e → ie, o → ue Stem-Changing Verbs** ✱

Actividad D La rutina de José

José works in a downtown office as a business manager. Indicate if he typically does the following activities in the morning (**por la mañana**), in the afternoon (**por la tarde**), or at night (**por la noche**).

		POR LA MAÑANA	POR LA TARDE	POR LA NOCHE
1.	Almuerza.	☐	☐	☐
2.	Duerme.	☐	☐	☐
3.	Se acuesta.	☐	☐	☐
4.	Empieza el trabajo.	☐	☐	☐
5.	Juega al tenis.	☐	☐	☐
6.	Se despierta.	☐	☐	☐
7.	Vuelve del trabajo.	☐	☐	☐

Actividad E ¿Bien preparados?

Paso 1 You will hear two students describe their study habits. After hearing what each one says, indicate if he will be well prepared for the exam.

	BIEN PREPARADO	NO MUY BIEN PREPARADO		BIEN PREPARADO	NO MUY BIEN PREPARADO
1.	☐	☐	4.	☐	☐
2.	☐	☐	5.	☐	☐
3.	☐	☐	6.	☐	☐

Paso 2 How well do you prepare for your exams? Check the sentence that best applies to you.

☐ Suelo prepararme muy bien para los exámenes.

☐ Suelo prepararme bastante bien para los exámenes.

☐ No suelo prepararme bien para los exámenes.

Actividad F ¿Pueden hacerlo (*do it*)?

Read the following statements that two friends make and decide if they can or cannot do what they want to do.

		SÍ	NO
1.	Queremos comprar un libro. Cuesta quince dólares y tenemos cincuenta.	☐	☐
2.	Queremos visitar un almacén. Cierran a las seis y ahora (*now*) son las cinco.	☐	☐
3.	Queremos ver una película en el cine. Empieza a las ocho y ahora son las diez.	☐	☐

	SÍ	NO
4. Queremos hablar con el profesor ahora mismo (*right now*). El profesor vuelve a su oficina a las tres y ahora son las dos.	☐	☐
5. Queremos hablar con un amigo en la cafetería. Suele almorzar a la una y nosotros almorzamos a las once.	☐	☐
6. Queremos llamar a una amiga. Ella se acuesta a las once y ahora son las nueve.	☐	☐

Go to page 61 to complete **¡Acción! 6.**

¡A escuchar!

Antes de escuchar

Paso 1 In a moment you will listen to Roberto and Marisela talking about **Episodio 2** of *Sol y viento*. On which aspect of this episode do you think they will concentrate? You will verify your answer after listening.

☐ Jaime's fortune: "Love is a whirlwind."

☐ Jaime's morning routine

☐ Jaime and María

Paso 2 Here are some new words and phrases you will encounter. Study them before listening.

pues	well, so
hacer buena pareja	to make a good match
tener cuidado	to be careful
mentir (ie)	to lie
demasiado	too much

A escuchar

Now listen to the conversation.

▲ Después de escuchar

Paso 1 Verify your answer to **Paso 1** of **Antes de escuchar.**

Paso 2 Answer the following questions based on what you heard.

1. Roberto y Marisela piensan que hay química entre Jaime y María.

   ☐ sí

   ☐ no

2. Marisela tiene una opinión favorable de Jaime.

   ☐ sí

   ☐ no

(continued)

3. ¿Cuántos años piensa Roberto que tienen Jaime y María? _____

4. ¿Cómo explica Roberto la «mentira» (*lie*) de Jaime?

   ☐ Cree que Jaime es una persona confiada.

   ☐ Piensa que Jaime es una persona privada.

   ☐ Cree que Jaime tiene prisa.

Estrategia

As you have learned in this lesson, some Spanish verbs have stem-vowel changes (e.g., **o → ue, e → ie, e → i,** and so forth). You can increase your chances of learning these verb forms by focusing your attention on them when you hear them used in the context of a conversation.

Paso 3 Listen to the exchange between Roberto and Marisela again. Use the strategy of listening for stem-changing verbs. First, write the stem-changing verb you hear. Then, write the infinitive form of the verb. Finally, specify the stem change that the verb underwent. The first one has been done for you.

	VERBO	INFINITIVO	CAMBIO (*CHANGE*)
1.	quieres	querer	e → ie
2.	_____	_____	_____
3.	_____	_____	_____
4.	_____	_____	_____
5.	_____	_____	_____
6.	_____	_____	_____
7.	_____	_____	_____

Paso 4 Now write two or three sentences about whether you agree with Roberto or with Marisela about the character Jaime.

VOCABULARIO ÚTIL

creo que...	I think that . . .
(No) Estoy de acuerdo.	I (don't) agree.
porque	because
(No) Tiene razón.	He/She is right (wrong).

_____

_____

_____

_____

_____

 ¡Acción!

¡Acción! 1 ¿Cuántos años tienen?

Write the names of five friends and/or family members and how old each person is. Then write a sentence that describes who is the oldest (_____ **es el/la mayor de todos**) and who is the youngest (_____ **es el/la menor de todos**).

    MODELO: Steve tiene treinta y seis años.

1. _____
2. _____
3. _____
4. _____
5. _____

    _____

    _____

¡Acción! 2 ¿Qué traes?

Write sentences telling what you bring with you when you go to the following places on or near campus. Use a dictionary to find words you don't know.

    MODELO: la cafetería → Traigo el carnet de estudiante (*student I.D.*).

1. la clase de español

    _____

2. la biblioteca

    _____

3. la clase de matemáticas

    _____

4. el cine

    _____

5. un concierto

    _____

6. una fiesta

    _____

¡Acción! 3 La brújula (*compass*)

Use the expressions **al norte de, al sur de, al este de,** and **al oeste de** to describe the position of the first continent in relation to the second. You can consult a map if you like.

    MODELO: Europa, Asia → Europa está al oeste de Asia.

  1. África, Europa

_____

  2. África, Sudamérica

_____

  3. Norteamérica, Europa

_____

  4. Asia, Europa

_____

  5. Sudamérica, Norteamérica

_____

  6. Australia, África

_____

¡Acción! 4 ¿Dónde están? ¿Qué están haciendo?

Answer the following questions with a complete sentence.

    MODELO: ¿Dónde está tu libro de español? → Está en el escritorio.

  1. ¿Dónde está tu mochila?

_____

  2. ¿Dónde están tus libros para las clases?

_____

  3. ¿Dónde están tus padres/hijos?

_____

  4. ¿Qué están haciendo tus padres/hijos en este momento?

_____

  5. ¿Qué estás haciendo tú en este momento?

_____

¡Acción! 5   ¿Adónde puede ir?

Write complete sentences to tell where tourists can go to do the following things.

> MODELO: comprar tabaco → El turista puede ir al estanco para (*in order to*) comprar tabaco.

1. correr o pasear con amigos

   _____

2. comprar recuerdos (*souvenirs*)

   _____

3. ver una película

   _____

4. dormir y descansar

   _____

5. cambiar (*to cash*) un cheque

   _____

6. tomar un autobús

   _____

¡Acción! 6   Tus metas (*goals*)

Paso 1   What are your goals? Write complete sentences to tell at least three things you want to achieve.

> MODELO: Quiero graduarme (*to graduate*) de la universidad.

1. _____
2. _____
3. _____

Paso 2   Choose one of your goals and describe in twenty-five to fifty words what you are in the habit of doing in order to work toward that goal.

> MODELO: Quiero graduarme de la universidad. Por eso (*Therefore*), suelo estudiar todos los
> días. También suelo...

_____

_____

_____

_____

_____

_____

_____

LECCIÓN **2B**

¡Vamos de compras!

OBJETIVOS

IN THIS LESSON, YOU WILL CONTINUE TO PRACTICE:

- **talking about what people are wearing**
- **stem-changing verbs in the present tense to talk about what people do**
- **numbers 100–1000**
- **using colors to describe clothing**
- **demonstrative adjectives and pronouns**
- **talking about shopping and making purchases**
- **ser and estar to talk about conditions and traits**

Vocabulario

La ropa

Clothing

 Actividad A   ¿Qué es?

You will hear a list of clothing items. Write the letter of the corresponding drawing for each item mentioned.

1. _____
2. _____
3. _____
4. _____
5. _____
6. _____
7. _____
8. _____
9. _____
10. _____

a.

b.

c.

d.

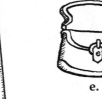
e.

f.

g.

h.

i.

j.

Actividad B ¡Busca al intruso!

Circle the item that does not belong.

1. **a.** el abrigo
   b. la chaqueta
   c. la gorra
   d. la sudadera

2. **a.** la blusa
   b. la falda
   c. el vestido
   d. la corbata

3. **a.** los pantalones
   b. los vaqueros
   c. los pantalones cortos
   d. las botas

4. **a.** los pantalones cortos
   b. el abrigo
   c. el traje de baño
   d. las sandalias

5. **a.** el vestido
   b. la sudadera
   c. el traje de baño
   d. los zapatos de tenis

6. **a.** las sandalias
   b. las botas
   c. la camiseta
   d. los zapatos de tenis

7. **a.** la camiseta
   b. los vaqueros
   c. la camisa
   d. la blusa

8. **a.** el traje de baño
   b. el traje
   c. el vestido
   d. la falda

Actividad C ¿Qué se pone primero?

Indicate the item of clothing that you typically put on first.

1. **a.** los zapatos
   b. los calcetines

2. **a.** la camiseta
   b. la chaqueta

3. **a.** el suéter
   b. el abrigo

4. **a.** los pantalones
   b. el cinturón (*belt*)

5. **a.** la camisa
   b. la corbata

6. **a.** la camiseta
   b. la sudadera

 Go to page 73 to complete ¡Acción! 1.

Gramática

Debo seguir.

e → i Stem-Changing Verbs

 Actividad D ¿A quién se refiere?

Listen to each statement and write the letter of the person(s) to whom it refers. Pay attention to the verb endings. You will hear each statement twice.

1. _____
2. _____
3. _____
4. _____
5. _____
6. _____

    a. yo (*the speaker*)
    b. tú (*the listener*)
    c. una estudiante
    d. nosotros
    e. tú y tus amigos (*in Spain*)
    f. los dependientes (*store clerks*)

Actividad E La ropa y las actividades

Match the activity or purpose with the most appropriate piece of clothing.

1. _____ Uno se viste con esto (*this*) para nadar (*swim*)

2. _____ Uno se viste con estos (*these*) para correr.

3. _____ Uno se viste con esto cuando hace frío.

4. _____ Uno se viste con esto para protegerse (*protect oneself*) del sol.

5. _____ Uno se viste con camiseta y estos cuando hace calor.

6. _____ Los hombres se visten con esto para un evento formal.

7. _____ Las mujeres se visten con esto para un evento formal.

a. el vestido
b. el abrigo
c. el traje
d. el traje de baño
e. los zapatos de tenis
f. los pantalones cortos
g. la gorra

  Go to page 73 to complete **¡Acción! 2.**

SEGUNDA PARTE

Vocabulario

Hay doscientas blusas rojas. **Colors; Numbers 100–1,000**

 ## Actividad A En la tienda

Listen to each statement about the prices of items in a store and write the letter of the corresponding number from the list in the blank. You will hear each statement twice.

1. _____
2. _____
3. _____
4. _____
5. _____
6. _____
7. _____
8. _____

a. 340
b. 315
c. 198
d. 210
e. 585
f. 125
g. 630
h. 120

Actividad B La ropa

Listen to each description and indicate the season, person, or occasion with which it corresponds. You will hear each description twice.

1. **a.** el invierno   **b.** el verano   **c.** el otoño

2. **a.** una fiesta (*party*)   **b.** el gimnasio   **c.** el parque (*park*)

3. **a.** el gimnasio   **b.** la oficina   **c.** un concierto de rock

4. **a.** el profesor de química **b.** una chica de cinco años **c.** un estudiante

5. **a.** el otoño   **b.** el invierno   **c.** la primavera

6. **a.** el invierno   **b.** el verano   **c.** el otoño

Actividad C ¿Qué color es?

Match each description with the corresponding color.

1. _____ la combinación de blanco y negro
2. _____ la combinación de rojo y amarillo
3. _____ la combinación de amarillo y azul
4. _____ la combinación de azul y rojo
5. _____ la combinación de blanco y rojo
6. _____ el cielo (*sky*) de día, el mar (*sea*)
7. _____ el cielo de noche, el funeral
8. _____ el algodón (*cotton*), la nieve (*snow*)

a. negro
b. verde
c. blanco
d. gris
e. azul
f. morado
g. anaranjado
h. rosado

 Go to page 74 to complete ¡Acción! 3.

Gramática

¿Qué es esto?   **Demonstrative Adjectives and Pronouns**

 Actividad D En la tienda

Listen to each sentence and determine which of the following sentences best describes what you hear.

1. **a.** La persona tiene los pantalones en la mano (*in hand*).   **b.** Otra persona tiene los pantalones.
2. **a.** La bolsa está enfrente de la persona.   **b.** La bolsa está lejos de la persona.
3. **a.** La persona se prueba unos zapatos.   **b.** Otra persona se prueba unos zapatos.
4. **a.** Las botas están en la tienda y la persona no.   **b.** La persona tiene las botas en la mano.
5. **a.** La persona tiene la blusa en la mano.   **b.** Otra persona tiene la blusa.
6. **a.** La persona se prueba el suéter.   **b.** Otra persona se prueba el suéter.

Actividad E ¿Cuáles?

Complete each exchange with the correct demonstrative pronoun.

1. —Necesito la falda de cuero (*leather*).
   —¿Cuál?
   a. Ese.   **b.** Esa.   **c.** Esos.   **d.** Esas.

2. —Deseo probarme unos zapatos de tenis.
   —¿Cuáles?
   a. Este.   **b.** Esta.   **c.** Estos.   **d.** Estas.

3. —Me gusta el cinturón (*belt*) negro.
   —¿Cuál?
   a. Aquel.   **b.** Aquella.   **c.** Aquellos.   **d.** Aquellas.

4. —¿Puedo probarme los pantalones blancos?
   —¿Cuáles?
   a. Este.   **b.** Esta.   **c.** Estos.   **d.** Estas.

5. —Prefiero el vestido morado.
   —¿Cuál?
   a. Ese.   **b.** Esa.   **c.** Esos.   **d.** Esas.

6. —¿Me puede traer las sandalias marrones?
   —¿Cuáles?
   a. Aquel.   **b.** Aquella.   **c.** Aquellos.   **d.** Aquellas.

Actividad F ¿Cuál es el tuyo?

Listen to each sentence and indicate the clothing item to which it corresponds.

1. **a.** el suéter   **b.** la bolsa   **c.** los pantalones
2. **a.** las sandalias   **b.** los zapatos   **c.** la blusa
3. **a.** el abrigo   **b.** los pantalones   **c.** la bufanda
4. **a.** la cartera   **b.** el abrigo   **c.** las sandalias
5. **a.** los calcetines   **b.** el vestido   **c.** la corbata
6. **a.** las botas   **b.** el vestido   **c.** la gorra
7. **a.** el abrigo   **b.** las gorras   **c.** los vaqueros
8. **a.** el traje   **b.** la chaqueta   **c.** los zapatos

 Go to page 74 to complete ¡Acción! 4.

TERCERA PARTE

Vocabulario

De compras   **Shopping**

Actividad A ¿En qué puedo servirle? (*How may I help you?*)

Put the following lines of an exchange between a clerk and a client in logical order by numbering them 1–9. The first two lines are numbered for you.

_____ DEPENDIENTE: Muy bien. Por aquí tenemos muchos. ¿Cuál es la talla de su mamá?

_____ DEPENDIENTE: ¿Qué tipo de vestido busca?

_____ DEPENDIENTE: Aquí hay uno en diez. ¿Le gusta este vestido? Es de las mejores (*best*) marcas y es una ganga.

_____ CLIENTE: Diez, creo. Y es muy baja.

___1___ DEPENDIENTE: Buenos días, señorita. ¿En qué puedo servirle?

_____ CLIENTE: ¡Excelente! Voy a comprar este. Pero, una pregunta, si le queda grande a mi mamá, ¿puedo devolver el vestido después?

_____ DEPENDIENTE: Sí, pero necesita traer el recibo (*receipt*). Vamos al mostrador, ¿no? ¿Desea pagar con tarjeta de crédito?

___2___ CLIENTE: Estoy buscando un vestido para mi mamá. Es su cumpleaños.

_____ CLIENTE: Un vestido elegante. Deseo ver los vestidos negros.

Actividad B Asociaciones

Listen to each description and then indicate the word or expression to which it corresponds. You will hear each description twice.

1. **a.** mediano   **b.** caro   **c.** pequeño

2. **a.** comprar   **b.** gastar   **c.** regatear

3. **a.** el dinero   **b.** la marca   **c.** la tarjeta de crédito

4. **a.** comprar   **b.** gastar   **c.** regatear

5. **a.** comprarme los pantalones   **b.** probarme los pantalones   **c.** vender los pantalones

6. **a.** una ganga   **b.** una talla   **c.** una tarjeta de crédito

7. **a.** la talla   **b.** el precio   **c.** la marca

Actividad C   ¿Qué venden?

Match each store with the items it sells.

1. _____ Zapatería González
2. _____ El Mundo (*World*) del Cuero (*Leather*)
3. _____ Todo Deporte
4. _____ Lana (*Wool*) Luxe
5. _____ Sastrería (*Tailor*) Gran Estilo
6. _____ El Mundo del Verano

a. las sudaderas y los zapatos de tenis
b. los trajes y las corbatas
c. los trajes de baño y las camisetas
d. las sandalias y las botas
e. los cinturones (*belts*) y las carteras
f. los suéteres y las bufandas (*scarves*)

 Go to page 75 to complete ¡**Acción!** **5.**

Gramática

Está bien.   **More on ser and estar**

Actividad D   ¿Esperado (*expected*) o inesperado (*unexpected*)?

Paso 1   Listen to the descriptions about Eduardo. Then indicate whether each statement describes something expected (**esperado**) or unexpected (**inesperado**).

	ESPERADO	INESPERADO
1.	☐	☐
2.	☐	☐
3.	☐	☐
4.	☐	☐
5.	☐	☐
6.	☐	☐
7.	☐	☐
8.	☐	☐

▲ **Paso 2**   Based on the descriptions from **Paso 1,** indicate the correct sentence.

☐ Normalmente Eduardo es una persona divertida, pero hoy está de mal humor (*in a bad mood*).

☐ Normalmente Eduardo es una persona difícil, pero hoy está de buen humor.

Actividad E ¿Un cambio (*change*) o una descripción?

Read each statement, then indicate if it is a reaction to a change (**cambio**) or if it is a description (**descripción**).

	CAMBIO	DESCRIPCIÓN
1. Marta tiene mucha ropa muy bonita. Es una mujer elegante.	☐	☐
2. Esos chicos están muy agresivos. Voy a llamar al director.	☐	☐
3. Paloma está muy grande.	☐	☐
4. Los estudiantes son un poco introvertidos en esa clase.	☐	☐
5. Después de un semestre en la universidad, estoy gordito (*chubby*).	☐	☐
6. Esos pantalones están muy feos (*ugly*).	☐	☐

Actividad F ¿Ser o estar?

Indicate the correct verb to complete each sentence.

	ES	ESTÁ
1. No me gusta ese programa. _____ aburrido.	☐	☐
2. Juana _____ muy pequeña. Puede comprar ropa en la sección para adolescentes.	☐	☐
3. No podemos comer ese tomate. _____ muy verde.	☐	☐
4. No me gusta hablar con José. _____ muy egoísta.	☐	☐
5. La camisa de Antonio _____ amarilla. ¡Muy amarilla!	☐	☐
6. Pepe no come bien y ahora (*now*) _____ muy delgado (*thin*).	☐	☐
7. Olga lleva ropa muy elegante hoy. _____ muy guapa (*good-looking*), ¿no?	☐	☐
8. La profesora necesita cancelar la clase porque _____ mal hoy.	☐	☐

 Go to page 76 to complete ¡**Acción!** 6.

 # Para escribir

Antes de escribir

For this activity, you will describe your first impressions of María and decide if she and Jaime have similar personalities. First, choose the adjectives from the list that best describe María, according to your first impressions. Then share your ideas with someone else.

(*continued*)

Creo que María es...

☐ aburrida.	☐ desconfiada.	☐ inteligente.
☐ alegre.	☐ divertida.	☐ introvertida.
☐ ambiciosa.	☐ enérgica.	☐ reservada.
☐ bonita (*pretty*).	☐ ingenua.	☐ seria.

A escribir

Paso 1 Now that you have made some preliminary decisions about your first impressions of María, decide how you will organize your thoughts. Select one of the possibilities below.

☐ describe each and then write about how María and Jaime are more similar than different

☐ describe each and then write about how María and Jaime are more different than similar

Paso 2 Now draft your composition on a separate sheet of paper. The following phrases may be helpful in writing your descriptions. You should also review the phrases from the **Para escribir** section of **Lección 1B** on page 43.

además	furthermore, in addition
creo que...	I think that . . .
me parece que...	it seems to me that . . .
(no) son (muy) parecidos	they're (not) (very) similar

Paso 3 Exchange compositions with a classmate so that you can provide initial feedback for each other. Do you agree with your classmate's assessment of Jaime's and María's personalities? As you read each other's composition, check for the following things.

☐ overall sense, meaning

☐ adjective/noun agreement

☐ subject/verb agreement

☐ spelling

Al entregar la composición

Paso 1 Review your classmate's feedback. As you go through your composition, remember to check for the correct use of the following.

☐ adjective/noun agreement

☐ subject/verb agreement

Paso 2 Now finalize your description and turn it in to your instructor.

 ¡Acción!

¡Acción! 1 La ropa

List at least three items of clothing for each category.

> MODELO: el verano → el traje de baño, las sandalias, los pantalones cortos

1. un hombre o una mujer de negocios (*businessman or businesswoman*)

   _____   _____

   _____   _____

2. el invierno en Minnesota

   _____   _____

   _____   _____

3. cuando llueve

   _____   _____

   _____   _____

4. un muchacho que practica el béisbol

   _____   _____

   _____   _____

5. la primavera en Nueva York

   _____   _____

   _____   _____

¡Acción! 2 Mis preferencias

Answer the following questions, based on your personal preferences. Use complete sentences. You may also use a dictionary to look up unfamiliar words.

1. ¿Cuál es tu restaurante favorito y qué sirven allí?

   _____

   _____

2. ¿Qué pides cuando vas a ese (*that*) restaurante?

   _____

   _____

(*continued*)

3. ¿Cómo te vistes para ir a la universidad, por lo general?

_____

_____

4. ¿Sigues la moda? ¿Qué marcas y tipo de ropa prefieres?

_____

_____

¡Acción! 3 Los uniformes

Write a sentence describing the typical color of the following uniforms. For the last item, describe the typical color of the uniform of another job or profession.

MODELO: la camisa del policía → La camisa del policía es azul.

1. la chaqueta del médico (_doctor_)

_____

2. la toga del juez (_judge's robe_)

_____

3. el hábito (_habit_) de la monja (_nun_)

_____

4. la camisa del árbitro (_referee_)

_____

5. la ropa que usa el soldado (_soldier_) como camuflaje

_____

6. otro

_____

¡Acción! 4 Esos y los míos

First, list five things that someone you know or someone around you is wearing. Then list five comparable things that you are wearing. Finally, compare what you and the other person are wearing, based on the model.

MODELO: él/ella lleva: camiseta   yo llevo: camiseta →
Esa camiseta no es como (_like_) la mía. La mía es verde y la suya es amarilla.

ÉL/ELLA LLEVA	YO LLEVO
1. _____	_____
_____	
2. _____	_____
_____	
3. _____	_____
_____	
4. _____	_____
_____	
5. _____	_____
_____	

¡Acción! 5 ¿Te gusta comprar en las tiendas o por el Internet?

Using some of the expressions below, write a paragraph explaining where you like to shop: in stores, on the Internet, both, or neither. Also explain why.

VOCABULARIO ÚTIL

devolver (ue)	to return (*something*)
las búsquedas	searches
el fraude	fraud
la presión	pressure
abierto/a	open
cerrado/a	closed

_____

_____

_____

_____

_____

_____

¡Acción! 6   ¿Qué te afecta?

Sometimes outside events can change our mood. Write six sentences in which you describe events or circumstances that change your moods.

MODELO: Soy bastante tranquila, pero cuando tengo un examen estoy muy nerviosa.

1. _____

2. _____

3. _____

4. _____

5. _____

6. _____

La familia

OBJETIVOS

IN THIS LESSON, YOU WILL CONTINUE TO PRACTICE:

- talking about members of your immediate and extended family

- talking about knowing people, places, and factual information using the verbs **saber** and **conocer**

- using object pronouns to eliminate redundancy

- describing how people look

- making comparisons to describe people and things

Vocabulario

Mi familia   **Members of the Immediate Family; Pets**

Actividad A La familia de Pilar

Indica si las siguientes (*following*) oraciones (*sentences*) son ciertas o falsas, según (*according to*) lo que dice Pilar de su familia. Puedes escuchar más de una vez si quieres.

		CIERTO	FALSO
1.	La hermanastra de Pilar se llama Teresa.	☐	☐
2.	Los gemelos tienen 22 años.	☐	☐
3.	Pilar no vive con su madre.	☐	☐
4.	El padre de Pilar ya murió (*already died*).	☐	☐
5.	Fanny es madre soltera.	☐	☐
6.	El gato de la familia se llama Osito.	☐	☐
7.	Pilar y Teresa tienen la misma edad.	☐	☐
8.	Clara es la hija adoptiva de Fanny.	☐	☐

Actividad B Las familias famosas

Indica qué relación existe (*exists*) entre las siguientes personas famosas.

1. Marge y Bart Simpson:

   a. hija/padre   **b.** madre/hijo   **c.** mujer/marido

2. Tom Cruise y Katie Holmes:

   a. esposo/esposa   **b.** hermano/hermana   **c.** hijo/madre

3. Ozzy y Kelly Osbourne:

   a. marido/mujer   **b.** hijo/madre   **c.** padre/hija

4. Mary-Kate y Ashley Olsen:

   a. hermanas adoptivas   **b.** hermanas gemelas   **c.** hermanastras

5. Nicole y Lionel Richie:

    a. hijastra/padre   **b.** mujer/marido   **c.** hija adoptiva/padre

6. Michael y Janet Jackson:

    a. hermano/hermana   **b.** padre/hija   **c.** hijo/madre

Actividad C Un árbol genealógico (*family tree*)

Estudia el siguiente árbol genealógico. Luego indica la(s) palabra(s) correcta(s) para completar cada una de las oraciones a continuación.

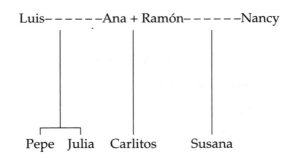

Luis– – – – – –Ana + Ramón– – – – – –Nancy

Pepe Julia Carlitos Susana

1. Carlitos es el _____ de Julia.

    a. hijo   **b.** medio hermano   **c.** padre

2. Julia y Pepe son los _____ de Ramón.

    a. hermanastros   **b.** hijos   **c.** hijastros

3. El padre soltero de esta familia se llama _____.

    a. Carlitos   **b.** Ramón   **c.** Luis

4. Ana es la _____ de Susana.

    a. madrastra   **b.** hijastra   **c.** madre

5. Pepe y Julia son _____.

    a. hermanos   **b.** hijos únicos   **c.** hermanastros

6. _____ son esposos.

    a. Ramón y Nancy   **b.** Ana y Ramón   **c.** Luis y Ana

 Go to page 91 to complete **¡Acción! 1.**

Gramática

Sí, conozco a la familia.
¿Sabes dónde están?

Saber and conocer;
Verbs that End in -zco

Actividad D ¿Sabes o conoces?

The following is a survey you could give a classmate to find out what he or she knows about the Spanish-speaking world. Indicate the correct verb form, **sabes** or **conoces,** to complete each question.

		SABES	CONOCES
1.	¿_____ quién descubrió América?	☐	☐
2.	¿_____ el arte de Salvador Dalí u otro pintor español?	☐	☐
3.	¿_____ la historia de *Don Quijote de la Mancha?*	☐	☐
4.	¿_____ la música de tango de Carlos Gardel?	☐	☐
5.	¿_____ en qué país se hablan el catalán y el vasco?	☐	☐
6.	¿_____ las bebidas (*drinks*) nacionales hispanas como el tequila, el ron o el jerez?	☐	☐

Actividad E ¿Es lógico o no?

▲ First, write the sentence that you hear. Then indicate if it is logical (**lógico**) or not (**ilógico**). You will hear each sentence twice.

		LÓGICO	ILÓGICO
1.	_____	☐	☐
2.	_____	☐	☐
3.	_____	☐	☐
4.	_____	☐	☐
5.	_____	☐	☐
6.	_____	☐	☐
7.	_____	☐	☐
8.	_____	☐	☐

Actividad F Situaciones

Indicate the correct verb to complete each sentence.

1. No _____ a mi padre porque él es alto (*tall*) y yo soy bajo (*short*).

   a. me parezco   **b.** obedezco

2. Si mi hermana no tiene dinero, yo _____ pagar sus cuentas.

   a. ofrezco   **b.** agradezco

3. No saludo (*I don't greet*) a una persona que no _____.

   a. merezco   **b.** reconozco

4. Cuando la profesora me ayuda (*helps me*) con la tarea, yo le _____ (*thank her*) mucho.

   a. reconozco   **b.** agradezco

5. No _____ una «A» en la clase de español porque siempre llego tarde a clase.

   a. ofrezco   **b.** merezco

6. Si no _____ a mis padres, ellos no me permiten (*allow me*) salir con mis amigos.

   a. obedezco   **b.** parezco

Go to page 91 to complete **¡Acción! 2.**

SEGUNDA PARTE

Vocabulario

Los otros parientes **Extended Family Members**

Actividad A La familia extendida

Empareja (*Match*) las definiciones con la palabra correcta.

1. _____ el esposo de tu hermana
2. _____ los padres de tu esposo/a
3. _____ los padres de tu madre
4. _____ el hermano de tu padre
5. _____ la hija de tu tía
6. _____ el hijo de tu hijo
7. _____ la hija de tu hermano
8. _____ la madre de tus primos

a. tu sobrina
b. tus suegros
c. tu cuñado
d. tu nieto
e. tus abuelos maternos
f. tu tía
g. tu prima
h. tu tío

Actividad B ¿Cierto o falso?

Escucha las oraciones e indica si son ciertas o falsas.

VOCABULARIO ÚTIL

el testamento   will

honrar   to honor

	CIERTO	FALSO
1.	☐	☐
2.	☐	☐
3.	☐	☐
4.	☐	☐
5.	☐	☐
6.	☐	☐

Actividad C Una familia extendida

Estudia el siguiente árbol genealógico. Luego, completa las oraciones a continuación con la palabra o los nombres correspondientes.

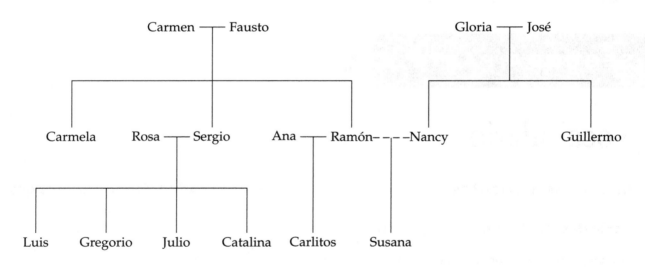

1. Catalina es la _____ de Carmen.

   a. abuela   **b.** sobrina   **c.** nieta

2. Ana y Carmela son _____.

   a. hermanas   **b.** cuñadas   **c.** suegras

3. Carmen y Fausto son los _____ de Rosa.

   a. suegros   **b.** padres   **c.** abuelos

4. Carlitos es el _____ de Gregorio.

   a. primo   **b.** tío   **c.** sobrino

5. Los abuelos maternos de Susana son _____.

   a. Ramón y Nancy   **b.** Carmen y Fausto   **c.** Gloria y José

6. Las tías de Carlitos son _____.

   a. Carmela y Ana   **b.** Rosa y Nancy   **c.** Carmela y Rosa

 Go to page 92 to complete **¡Acción! 3.**

Gramática

¿La conoce?   **Direct Object Pronouns**

Actividad D   **¿Quién hace qué?**

Listen to each sentence and indicate the sentence in English that corresponds with it.

1. ☐ Marisol understands him well.

   ☐ He understands Marisol well.

2. ☐ Juan sees them frequently.

   ☐ They see Juan frequently.

3. ☐ She wants to invite Jorge.

   ☐ Jorge wants to invite her.

4. ☐ Griselda knows César.

   ☐ César knows Griselda.

5. ☐ He respects her a lot.

   ☐ She respects him a lot.

6. ☐ They hug her.

   ☐ She hugs them.

7. ☐ Alejandro listens to him.

   ☐ He listens to Alejandro.

8. ☐ They criticize their mother.

   ☐ Their mother criticizes them.

Actividad E ¿A quién se refiere?

Indicate to whom each of the following sentences refers.

1. La llamo con frecuencia.
   a. mi tía
   b. mi hermano
   c. mi primo

2. Los veo los viernes.
   a. mis amigas
   b. mis abuelos
   c. mis hermanastras

3. Lo quiero mucho.
   a. mi madrastra
   b. mi gato
   c. mi cuñada

4. Las adoro (*I adore*).
   a. mis tíos
   b. mis suegros
   c. mis abuelas

5. La respeto (*I respect*).
   a. mi vecino (*neighbor*)
   b. mi mascota
   c. mi compañero de clase

6. Lo visito en enero.
   a. mi profesora
   b. mi amiga
   c. mi consejero (*advisor*)

Actividad F ¿Quién a quién?

Indicate the sentence in English that corresponds to each sentence in Spanish.

1. La llama un hombre.

   ☐ A man is calling her.

   ☐ She is calling a man.

2. A mi madre la besa mi padre.

   ☐ My mother kisses my father.

   ☐ My father kisses my mother.

3. La busca un niño.

   ☐ She is looking for a child.

   ☐ A child is looking for her.

4. Nos ayudan nuestros padres.

   ☐ Our parents help us.

   ☐ We help our parents.

5. Lo quiere llamar ella.

   ☐ She wants to call him.

   ☐ He wants to call her.

6. Los detestan los niños.

   ☐ They detest the children.

   ☐ The children detest them.

 Go to page 92 to complete ¡Acción! 4.

TERCERA PARTE

Vocabulario

No es muy alto.

Physical Traits

Actividad A El pelo

Indica la palabra correcta para completar cada oración.

1. _____ Una persona sin pelo es…

2. _____ Demi Moore tiene el pelo…

3. _____ Julianne Moore es…

4. _____ Shirley Temple tenía (*had*) el pelo…

5. _____ Tiger Woods tiene el pelo rizado y…

6. _____ Con los años el pelo tiende a (*tends*) ser…

a. rizado.
b. canoso.
c. pelirroja.
d. calva.
e. largo.
f. corto.

Actividad B ¿Quién es?

Escucha las descripciones e indica la persona descrita (*described*).

1. **a.** George Clooney
   b. Woody Allen

2. **a.** Renée Zellweger
   b. Rosie O'Donnell

3. **a.** Keanu Reeves
   b. Robert Redford

4. **a.** Susan Sarandon
   b. Nicole Kidman

5. **a.** Brad Pitt
   b. John Malkovich

6. **a.** Madonna
   b. Minnie Driver

Actividad C ¿Lógico o ilógico?

Indica si las siguientes oraciones son lógicas o ilógicas.

		LÓGICO	ILÓGICO
1.	Para ser jinete (*jockey*) profesional, es bueno ser alto.	☐	☐
2.	Las personas con la piel muy blanca deben pasar mucho tiempo al sol.	☐	☐
3.	Los soldados (*soldiers*) suelen tener el pelo muy corto.	☐	☐
4.	Por lo general, las modelos* de ropa son delgadas.	☐	☐
5.	Los niños suelen ser canosos.	☐	☐
6.	El pelo rojo y las pecas son características físicas típicas de los hispanos.	☐	☐

 Go to page 93 to complete **¡Acción! 5.**

Gramática

Es más alto que yo. **Comparisons of Equality and Inequality**

Actividad D ¿Más o menos?

Indicate the correct word to complete each sentence.

1. California es _____ grande que Ohio.

   ☐ más   ☐ menos

2. La población de Alaska es _____ numerosa que la de Nueva York.

   ☐ más   ☐ menos

3. George W. Bush es _____ que George Bush.

   ☐ mayor   ☐ menor

4. El número de hispanohablantes es _____ en Florida que en Maine.

   ☐ mayor   ☐ menor

5. En las universidades de los Estados Unidos, hay _____ estudiantes de español que de árabe (*Arabic*).

   ☐ más   ☐ menos

6. El mes de mayo tiene _____ días que el mes de noviembre.

   ☐ más   ☐ menos

---

*The word **modelo** is invariable in form and is used whether talking about a male model or a female model.

Actividad E ¿Cierto o falso?

Listen to Lidia describe her family. Then indicate whether each sentence is true (**cierto**) or false (**falso**), based on what she says. You can listen more than once if you like.

VOCABULARIO ÚTIL

parecidas	similar
de mal humor	in a bad mood
no se lleva bien	doesn't get along well

	CIERTO	FALSO
1. Luz es menor que Ricardo.	☐	☐
2. A Luz y Eva les gustan más los deportes que a Lidia.	☐	☐
3. Teresa es mayor que Lidia.	☐	☐
4. Clara tiene tantos años como Lidia.	☐	☐
5. Clara es la menos simpática de la familia.	☐	☐
6. Raúl es el menor de la familia.	☐	☐

Actividad F En el mundo

Indicate the correct word to complete each sentence.

1. La ciudad de Chicago es _____ interesante como la ciudad de Nueva York.

   a. tanto **b.** tan **c.** tanta

2. Hay _____ tráfico en Barcelona como en la ciudad de México.

   a. tanto **b.** tanta **c.** tan

3. En Madrid, los adolescentes no trabajan _____ como los adolescentes en Pittsburgh.

   a. tan **b.** tanto **c.** tantos

4. Los trenes en los Estados Unidos no van _____ rápido como los trenes en Europa.

   a. tantos **b.** tanto **c.** tan

5. Hay _____ montañas (*mountains*) altas en Chile como en Colorado.

   a. tantos **b.** tan **c.** tantas

6. No hay _____ violencia en el campo (*country*) como en la ciudad.

   a. tan **b.** tanto **c.** tanta

 Go to page 93 to complete **¡Acción! 6.**

¡A escuchar!

Antes de escuchar

Paso 1 Ahora Roberto y Marisela hablan del **Episodio 3** de *Sol y viento*. Específicamente, hablan de Carlos y Jaime. Indica las oraciones a continuación que corresponden a lo que tú crees que Roberto y Marisela piensan de Carlos y Jaime. Vas a averiguar (*check*) tus respuestas (*answers*) después de escuchar su conversación.

☐ A Marisela no le gusta la actitud (*attitude*) de Carlos.

☐ Roberto piensa que Carlos es un buen hombre de negocios.

☐ Roberto y Marisela piensan que Carlos no trata (*treat*) bien a sus empleados.

☐ Roberto cree que Jaime está preocupado (*worried*).

☐ Marisela opina que Carlos no quiere (*doesn't love*) a su madre.

Paso 2 Estudia las siguientes palabras y frases que se usan en esta conversación.

mentiroso	deceitful
tratar	to treat
el jefe	boss
cansado	tired
de todas maneras	anyway, anyhow
presionar	to pressure
por cierto	by the way
distraído	distracted

 ## A escuchar

Ahora, escucha la conversación.

▲ Después de escuchar

Paso 1 Averigua tus respuestas para **Antes de escuchar, Paso 1** en la clave de respuestas (*answer key*).

Paso 2 Ahora contesta cada pregunta a continuación, basándote en (*based on*) lo que oíste (*you heard*).

1. Marisela tiene una opinión más favorable de Carlos que de Jaime.

   ☐ sí

   ☐ no

2. Roberto piensa que Carlos está...

   ☐ preocupado y exagerado.

   ☐ cansado y serio.

   ☐ nervioso y preocupado.

3. Según Roberto, la hermana de Carlos es menor que Carlos.

   ☐ sí

   ☐ no

4. Roberto cree que Jaime también tiene preocupaciones porque...

   ☐ está nervioso.

   ☐ está serio y distraído.

   ☐ habla de su familia.

Estrategia

Remember to use **más... que** and **menos... que** to make unequal comparisons in Spanish. When making comparisons of equality use **tan/tanto... como**. The words **mayor** and **menor** are used to compare ages.

Paso 3 Escucha la conversación entre Roberto y Marisela otra vez. Usa la estrategia y trata de reconocer las comparaciones.

1. Escoge (*Choose*) una comparación con la que (*with which*) estás de acuerdo y escríbela en el espacio en blanco.

   _____

2. Ahora escoge una comparación con la que *no* estás de acuerdo y escríbela en el espacio en blanco.

   _____

3. Corrige (*Correct*) la segunda comparación para expresar tu propia (*own*) opinión.

   _____

(continued)

Paso 4 Ahora escribe dos o tres oraciones sobre lo que piensas de la opinión de Roberto sobre Carlos.

_____

_____

_____

_____

_____

_____

 ¡Acción!

¡Acción! 1 Una prueba

Dibuja (*Draw*) el árbol genealógico de tu familia. Luego, escribe seis oraciones, algunas ciertas y otras falsas, basadas en el árbol. Tu profesor(a) va a indicar si tus oraciones son ciertas o falsas.

Los _____

MODELO: Gloria es mi madre.

		CIERTO	FALSO
1. _____.		☐	☐
2. _____.		☐	☐
3. _____.		☐	☐
4. _____.		☐	☐
5. _____.		☐	☐
6. _____.		☐	☐

¡Acción! 2 Preguntas para mi profesor(a)

Escribe tres oraciones con **saber** y tres oraciones con **conocer** para conseguir (*get*) información sobre tu profesor(a) de español. Usa **tú** o **Ud.,** según la costumbre (*custom*) de la clase.

MODELO: ¿Sabe Ud. tocar algún instrumento musical?

1. _____.

2. _____.

3. _____.

4. _____.

5. _____.

6. _____.

¡Acción! 3 Mi familia extendida

Escribe un párrafo de más o menos cincuenta palabras sobre tu familia extendida. Incluye información sobre tus tíos, abuelos, primos, etcétera.

_____

_____

_____

_____

_____

_____

_____

_____

_____

_____

¡Acción! 4 Los parientes

Paso 1 Utilizando los verbos a continuación, escribe tres oraciones en las que describes lo que los parientes nos hacen (*do for us*). Usa otras palabras para aumentar (*enhance*) tus oraciones.

abrazar   invitar

comprender   llamar (por teléfono)

conocer   respetar

escuchar

MODELO: Nos llaman por teléfono con frecuencia (*frequently*).

1. _____

2. _____

3. _____

Paso 2 Ahora escribe tres oraciones sobre lo que nosotros les hacemos (*do for*) a nuestros parientes. Utiliza los mismos verbos del **Paso 1**.

MODELO: Los invitamos a nuestra casa para la Navidad (*Christmas*).

1. _____

2. _____

3. _____

¡Acción! 5   ¿Cómo es?

Escribe una oración para describir a cada persona a continuación. Incluye por lo menos tres rasgos físicos.

1. (yo) _____

   _____.

2. (mi mejor amigo/a) _____

   _____.

3. (mi profesor[a] de español) _____

   _____.

4. (mi actor favorito) _____

   _____.

5. (mi actriz favorita) _____

   _____.

6. (un pariente) _____

   _____.

¡Acción! 6   Comparaciones

Escribe seis oraciones en las que te comparas (*you compare yourself*) con diferentes miembros de tu familia.

más que	mayor que	tan… como
menos que	menor que	tanto/a(s)… como

MODELO: Mi hermano no tiene tantos gatos como yo.

1. _____
2. _____
3. _____
4. _____
5. _____
6. _____

¡A comer!

OBJETIVOS

IN THIS LESSON, YOU WILL CONTINUE TO PRACTICE:

- **talking about what you eat for breakfast**

- **expressing negation**

- **talking about what you eat for lunch and for snacking**

- **contrasting the uses of ser and estar**

- **talking about what you eat for dinner**

- **using indirect object pronouns**

Vocabulario

El desayuno

Breakfast

Actividad A Asociaciones

Empareja cada comida con la categoría correspondiente.

1. _____ la rosquilla
2. _____ el tocino
3. _____ el yogur
4. _____ los huevos
5. _____ el cereal
6. _____ la salchicha
7. _____ la toronja
8. _____ el pan tostado

a. frutas y verduras
b. productos lácteos (*dairy*)
c. carbohidratos
d. proteínas

Actividad B Mis desayunos

Indica si las siguientes oraciones son ciertas o falsas según lo que dice Marisol sobre sus desayunos. Puedes escuchar más de una vez si quieres.

Marisol…

		CIERTO	FALSO
1.	come panqueques los días de trabajo.	☐	☐
2.	come cereal como parte de su dieta los jueves.	☐	☐
3.	desayuna yogur los fines de semana.	☐	☐
4.	come una barra de frutas en el autobús.	☐	☐
5.	come proteínas los fines de semana.	☐	☐
6.	desayuna cereal los miércoles.	☐	☐
7.	toma café todos los días.	☐	☐
8.	come huevos los fines de semana.	☐	☐

Actividad C El desayuno preferido

Escucha cada una de las oraciones e indica el desayuno correspondiente de la lista. Vas a oír cada oración dos veces.

1. _____
2. _____
3. _____
4. _____
5. _____
6. _____

a. café con leche o jugo
b. pan tostado a la francesa con jarabe (*syrup*), huevos fritos, tocino, café y jugo de naranja
c. cereal cocido y café
d. media toronja y una manzana
e. yogur y un vaso de leche
f. chilaquiles y salchichas

Go to page 107 to complete ¡**Acción!** 1.

Gramática

No lo sé tampoco.   Indefinite and Negative Words

Actividad D ¿Qué tipo de estudiante es?

Indicate whether each statement refers to a good student (**bueno**) or a bad student (**malo**).

	BUENO	MALO
1. Jamás hace la tarea.	☐	☐
2. Nunca llega tarde a clases.	☐	☐
3. No hace nada en clase.	☐	☐
4. No se lleva bien (*He/She doesn't get along well*) con nadie.	☐	☐
5. Si alguien necesita ayuda, siempre se la ofrece (*offers it to him/her*).	☐	☐
6. Nunca participa en ninguna actividad de la clase.	☐	☐
7. Siempre come o bebe algo en sus clases.	☐	☐
8. Nunca entrega nada tarde.	☐	☐

Actividad E ¿Qué tipo de profesor es?

Listen to the descriptions of two different Spanish professors. Indicate whether each description refers to a good professor (**bueno**) or a bad professor (**malo**).

VOCABULARIO ÚTIL

se siente frustrado	he/she feels frustrated
sin	without
de antemano	beforehand

	BUENO	MALO
1.	☐	☐
2.	☐	☐
3.	☐	☐
4.	☐	☐
5.	☐	☐
6.	☐	☐
7.	☐	☐
8.	☐	☐

Actividad F La importancia del desayuno

Circle the correct words in parentheses to complete the following paragraph about the importance of eating breakfast.

(**Siempre / Nunca**)[1] se dice que el desayuno es la comida más importante del día. Los expertos dicen que debemos consumir el 25 por ciento de las calorías del día por la mañana. La mayoría de las personas[a] no tiene (**algo / nada**)[2] en contra de tal[b] afirmación, pero la verdad es que muchas personas (**siempre / jamás**)[3] desayunan por falta[c] de tiempo. Los que sí[d] tienen tiempo no tienen (**alguna / ninguna**)[4] motivación para comer una dieta equilibrada.[e] Suelen seleccionar comidas altas en azúcar como *Pop Tarts,* panqueques y pasteles. (**También / Tampoco**)[5] desayunan comidas altas en grasas, como las de los restaurantes de comida rápida. Así parece que es necesario que (**alguien / nadie**)[6] nos vuelva a enseñar[f] cómo desayunar saludablemente.

[a]La... *Most people* [b]en... *against such* [c]*lack* [d]Los... *Those who do* [e]*balanced* [f]nos... *teach us again*

Go to page 107 to complete ¡**Acción! 2.**

SEGUNDA PARTE

Vocabulario

El almuerzo y la merienda   **Lunch and Snacking**

✳

Actividad A Categorías

Indica el alimento que corresponde a cada una de las categorías de comida.

1. los dulces

   a. la chuleta   **b.** el bróculi   **c.** el helado

2. las proteínas

   a. las galletas   **b.** el pescado   **c.** las papas

3. los productos lácteos

   a. los frijoles   **b.** el queso   **c.** el bistec

4. las verduras

   a. las zanahorias   **b.** el pollo   **c.** la toronja

5. los carbohidratos

   a. la lechuga   **b.** la salsa   **c.** el arroz

6. los postres

   a. el flan   **b.** la hamburguesa   **c.** la sopa

Actividad B ¿Almuerzo mexicano o norteamericano?

Escucha cada descripción e indica si corresponde a un almuerzo al estilo mexicano o norteamericano.

	MEXICANO	NORTEAMERICANO
1.	☐	☐
2.	☐	☐
3.	☐	☐
4.	☐	☐
5.	☐	☐
6.	☐	☐

Actividad C Preguntas alimenticias (*food*)

Lee cada pregunta e indica la respuesta correcta.

1. ¿Cuál de los siguientes alimentos es bajo en calorías?

   a. el sándwich de verduras   **b.** la chuleta de cerdo   **c.** las papas fritas

2. ¿Cuál de los siguientes platos es ideal para un vegetariano?

   a. el jamón   **b.** la ensalada   **c.** el pollo

3. ¿Qué no debe consumir un diabético?

   a. sándwiches de carnes   **b.** verduras con mantequilla   **c.** refrescos con azúcar

4. Si uno está a dieta (*on a diet*), ¿qué debe evitar (*avoid*)?

   a. el bróculi   **b.** el helado   **c.** los jalapeños

5. ¿Qué se recomienda tomar cuando uno hace ejercicio (*exercises*)?

   a. cerveza   **b.** vino   **c.** agua

6. ¿Cuál de las siguientes comidas suele servirse caliente?

   a. la sopa   **b.** el sándwich con mermelada   **c.** la toronja

 Go to page 107 to complete **¡Acción! 3.**

Gramática

Está muy serio.   **Ser Versus estar with Adjectives**

 Actividad D ¿Ser o estar?

Listen to each statement and indicate whether it refers to an inherent condition (**condición inherente**) or a variable condition (**condición variable**).

	CONDICIÓN INHERENTE	CONDICIÓN VARIABLE
1.	☐	☐
2.	☐	☐
3.	☐	☐
4.	☐	☐
5.	☐	☐
6.	☐	☐

Actividad E ¿Está bien cocido?

Indicate the correct phrase with **estar** to complete each sentence.

1. La cerveza, después de pasar unas horas en el refrigerador,...

   a. está cruda. **b.** está pasada. **c.** está fría.

2. Los chiles jalapeños, cuando se comen muy maduros (*ripe*),...

   a. están salados. **b.** están picantes. **c.** están calientes.

3. Las fresas (*strawberries*), cuando se comen muy rojas,...

   a. están cocidas. **b.** están agrias. **c.** están dulces.

4. El té, sin (*without*) azúcar ni miel (*honey*),...

   a. está frío. **b.** está amargo. **c.** está caliente.

5. La sopa, cuando no tiene sabor (*taste*),...

   a. está picosa. **b.** está aguada. **c.** está agria.

6. El bistec, cuando tiene un color rojizo (*reddish*),...

   a. está pasado. **b.** está caliente. **c.** está crudo.

Actividad F Un diálogo

Circle the correct form of **ser** or **estar** in parentheses to complete the following dialogue between a waiter (**el mesero**) and a restaurant patron (**el cliente**).

MESERO: ¿Qué tal (**es/está**)[1] la comida hoy, señor?

CLIENTE: El bistec suele (**ser/estar**)[2] muy rico aquí, pero hoy (**es/está**)[3] muy crudo.

MESERO: Le puedo traer otro. Seguro que le gustan las verduras... (**son/están**)[4] las más frescas[a] de la región.

CLIENTE: Por lo general sí, pero estas (**son/están**)[5] duras y pasadas.

MESERO: Mil disculpas.[b] ¿Y la sopa, señor?

CLIENTE: Bueno, (**es/está**)[6] caliente y muy rica, ¡pero no (**es/está**)[7] lo que pedí![c]

[a]*fresh* [b]*Mil... A thousand pardons.* [c]*lo... what I ordered*

  Go to page 108 to complete **¡Acción! 4.**

Vocabulario

La cena

 Dinner

Actividad A ¿Qué es?

Escucha cada definición e indica el alimento o la bebida correspondiente.

1. **a.** el maíz   **b.** la lechuga   **c.** los espárragos
2. **a.** la cerveza   **b.** el vino   **c.** el refresco
3. **a.** el plátano   **b.** la manzana   **c.** la toronja
4. **a.** la coliflor   **b.** el flan   **c.** el pastel
5. **a.** la papa   **b.** el tomate   **c.** la zanahoria
6. **a.** el té   **b.** la cerveza   **c.** el refresco

Actividad B ¿De qué marca es?

Empareja cada alimento o bebida con la marca correspondiente.

1. _____ el pastel
2. _____ la sopa
3. _____ la cerveza
4. _____ las verduras congeladas (*frozen*)
5. _____ los espaguetis
6. _____ el aceite de maíz
7. _____ el jamón
8. _____ el helado

a. Wesson
b. Green Giant
c. Oscar Meyer
d. Heineken
e. Campbell's
f. Sara Lee
g. Ben & Jerry's
h. Barilla

Actividad C ¡Busca el intruso!

Indica la comida que *no* se asocia con cada categoría a continuación.

1. los mariscos

   a. la langosta   **b.** el camarón   **c.** el pollo

2. las grasas

   a. el arroz   **b.** la mantequilla   **c.** el tocino

3. las carnes

   a. el rosbif   **b.** el queso   **c.** la chuleta de cerdo

4. los postres

   a. las papas   **b.** el pastel   **c.** el helado

5. las frutas

   a. la manzana   **b.** la banana   **c.** la lechuga

6. las verduras

   a. el maíz   **b.** la zanahoria   **c.** el pan

7. los carbohidratos

   a. el arroz   **b.** la toronja   **c.** la galleta

8. los productos lácteos

   a. el aguacate   **b.** la mantequilla   **c.** el queso

 Go to page 108 to complete **¡Acción! 5.**

Gramática

¿Le gusta el vino?   **Indirect Object Pronouns and gustar**

 Actividad D   ¿Qué le gusta?

Listen to the speakers describe some preferences they have regarding meals. Then indicate the letter of the food item(s) to complete each of the following sentences.

1. A esta persona probablemente le gustan…

   a. las papas fritas.   **b.** las verduras.   **c.** los pasteles.

2. A esta persona probablemente le gusta…

   a. el helado.   **b.** la sopa.   **c.** la leche.

3. A esta persona probablemente *no* le gusta…

   a. el aguacate.   **b.** la carne de res.   **c.** la hamburguesa de soja.

4. A esta persona probablemente le gustan…

   a. los espaguetis.   **b.** las tortillas.   **c.** las zanahorias.

5. A esta persona probablemente *no* le gusta…

   a. el agua.   **b.** el jugo.   **c.** la cerveza.

6. A esta persona probablemente le gusta…

   a. el rosbif.   **b.** la ensalada.   **c.** el pescado.

Actividad E En el restaurante

Indicate the order, from 1–7, in which a waiter does the following things for clients in a restaurant.

El mesero (*waiter*)…

_____ nos trae el aperitivo (*appetizer*) y nos toma el orden (*order*).

_____ nos pregunta si un aperitivo deseamos.

_____ nos da la cuenta.

_____ nos dice «Bienvenidos» (*Welcome*).

_____ nos da el menú.

_____ nos ofrece el postre.

_____ nos da las gracias y nos invita a volver al restaurante.

Actividad F ¿Le o les?

Indicate the correct indirect object pronoun (**le** or **les**) to complete each sentence.

1. Los diabéticos no _____ ponen azúcar al cereal preparado.
   - ☐ le
   - ☐ les

2. Los niños _____ ponen mucha salsa de tomate (*ketchup*) a las papas fritas.
   - ☐ le
   - ☐ les

3. Mucha gente _____ pone mayonesa a los sándwiches.
   - ☐ le
   - ☐ les

4. Uno _____ puede poner hielo (*ice*) a la sopa si está muy caliente.
   - ☐ le
   - ☐ les

5. En Chicago _____ ponen tomates picados (*diced*) a los perros calientes (*hot dogs*).
   - ☐ le
   - ☐ les

6. Si uno _____ pone cebollas al sándwich de atún, debe masticar chicle (*chew gum*) después para no tener mal aliento (*bad breath*).
   - ☐ le
   - ☐ les

Go to page 109 to complete **¡Acción! 6.**

Para escribir

Antes de escribir

Para esta actividad, vas a escribir una breve composición sobre los gustos de Jaime y Carlos. Para comenzar, indica si las oraciones se refieren a Jaime, a Carlos o a los dos.

	JAIME	CARLOS	LOS DOS
1. Le gusta darse aires (*put on airs*).	☐	☐	☐
2. Le gusta su trabajo (*work*).	☐	☐	☐
3. Le gusta mandar (*give orders*).	☐	☐	☐
4. No le gusta esperar (*to wait*).	☐	☐	☐
5. Le gusta ir al grano (*to get to the point*).	☐	☐	☐
6. Le gustan los vinos chilenos.	☐	☐	☐
7. Le gustan los negocios (*business*).	☐	☐	☐
8. No le gustan las sorpresas (*surprises*).	☐	☐	☐

A escribir

Paso 1 Ahora que tienes ideas sobre los gustos de cada personaje, ¿cómo vas a organizarlas? Escoge una de las posibilidades a continuación.

☐ escribir sobre los gustos de Jaime primero, y luego sobre los de Carlos

☐ escribir sobre los gustos de Carlos, y luego sobre los de Jaime

☐ comparar a los dos simultáneamente, según la lista de características

Paso 2 Ahora escribe un borrador (*rough draft*) en una hoja (*sheet*) de papel aparte. Las palabras y frases a continuación te pueden ser útiles al redactar (*upon writing*) tu composición.

por otro (lado)	on the other (hand)
por un lado	on the one hand
también	also
tampoco	either, neither

Paso 3 Intercambia tu composición con la de un compañero (una compañera) de clase. Mientras lees su composición, revisa los siguientes puntos.

☐ el significado y el sentido en general

☐ la concordancia (*agreement*) entre sustantivo y adjetivo

☐ la concordancia entre sujeto y verbo

☐ la ortografía (*spelling*)

Al entregar la composición

Usa los comentarios de tu compañero/a de clase para escribir una versión final de tu composición. Repasa (*Review*) los siguientes puntos sobre el lenguaje y luego entrégale la composición a tu profesor(a).

- ☐ el uso correcto de **le** y **les**

- ☐ el uso correcto de **gusta** y **gustan**

🎬 ¡Acción!

¡Acción! 1   ¿Qué desayunas?

Escribe un párrafo de más o menos cincuenta palabras sobre lo que comes para el desayuno los días de entre semana (*on weekdays*). ¿Crees que tus desayunos son típicos de un estudiante de tu universidad?

_____

_____

_____

_____

_____

_____

¡Acción! 2   ¿Desayunas algo?

Escribe seis oraciones sobre lo que comes o no comes por la mañana. Usa expresiones indefinidas y negativas en tus oraciones.

    MODELO: No desayuno cereal nunca.

1. _____
2. _____
3. _____
4. _____
5. _____
6. _____

¡Acción! 3   El almuerzo ideal

Describe el almuerzo ideal para cada una de las personas descritas (*described*) a continuación.

    MODELO: una mujer embarazada (*pregnant*) →
          El almuerzo ideal para una mujer embarazada es un vaso de leche, un sándwich de pavo y fruta.

1. un jugador de fútbol americano

_____

2. una supermodelo

_____

3. un niño (una niña) de 5 años

_____

(*continued*)

4. un hombre (una mujer) de negocios (*businessman/woman*)

_____

5. un(a) adolescente

_____

6. un vegetariano

_____

¡Acción! 4   Adivinanzas (*Riddles*)

Escoge seis alimentos de esta lección y escribe una adivinanza para cada uno, usando **ser** y **estar.** Usa **estar** en por lo menos dos de las adivinanzas. Incluye la respuesta a las adivinanzas entre paréntesis.

MODELOS: Esta verdura **es** anaranjada y puede comerse cocida o cruda. ¿Qué es?
(la zanahoria)
Esta proteína **es** dura cuando **está** muy bien cocida. ¿Qué es? (el bistec)

1. _____
_____

2. _____
_____

3. _____
_____

4. _____
_____

5. _____
_____

6. _____
_____

¡Acción! 5   Los días festivos (*Holidays*)

Completa las siguientes oraciones con alimentos y bebidas que normalmente cenas en el día indicado. Si no celebras algún día, indica otro día de celebración.

MODELO: Suelo cenar bistec, espárragos con mantequilla y vino tinto para la Nochebuena
(*Christmas Eve*).

1. Para la Nochebuena suelo cenar _____, _____ y _____.

2. El Día de Acción de Gracias (*Thanksgiving*) me gusta cenar _____, _____ y _____.

3. Para la Noche Vieja (*New Year's Eve*) suelo cenar _____, _____ y _____.

4. Para celebrar la Pascua (*Easter*) suelo cenar _____, _____ y _____.

5. En una primera cita (*first date*) nunca ceno _____, _____ o _____.

6. Para celebrar mi cumpleaños (*birthday*) suelo cenar _____ y _____ pero no ceno

_____ ese día.

¡Acción! 6 Mi profesor(a) de español

Escribe seis oraciones sobre lo que crees que le gusta o no le gusta comer y beber a tu profesor(a) de español. Tu profesor(a) puede indicar si tienes razón (*if you're right*) o no.

MODELOS: A mi profesora le gustan mucho los mariscos.

A mi profesor no le gusta el vino.

		SÍ	NO
1.	_____	☐	☐
2.	_____	☐	☐
3.	_____	☐	☐
4.	_____	☐	☐
5.	_____	☐	☐
6.	_____	☐	☐

LECCIÓN **4A**

Cuando no trabajo...

OBJETIVOS

IN THIS LESSON, YOU WILL CONTINUE TO PRACTICE:

- **talking about pastimes and leisure activities**

- **talking about sports and fitness activities**

- **talking about special occasions and holidays**

- **talking about activities in the past using the preterite tense**

Vocabulario

El tiempo libre   **Leisure Activities**

 Actividad A **Descripciones**

Escucha los verbos y empareja cada uno con la descripción correspondiente. Vas a oír cada verbo dos veces.

1. _____ Es el acto de hacer figuras e imágenes con un lápiz y una hoja de papel.

2. _____ Es una actividad de concentración y descanso (*rest*) mental.

3. _____ Es participar en un juego de estrategia.

4. _____ Es una actividad que consiste en pasar la vista por (*to look over*) lo escrito en un libro, un periódico u otro texto.

5. _____ Es lo que haces cuando la casa está desordenada (*messy*) o en malas condiciones.

6. _____ Necesitas ritmo y coordinación para hacer esto bien.

7. _____ Esta actividad consiste en preparar comida.

8. _____ Esto se hace en Blockbuster o con Netflix.

Actividad B Asociaciones

Empareja cada verbo con el objeto correspondiente.

1. _____ pintar
2. _____ leer
3. _____ cocinar
4. _____ andar
5. _____ tocar
6. _____ jugar
7. _____ dar
8. _____ coleccionar

a. en bicicleta
b. fiestas
c. el piano
d. un retrato (*portrait*)
e. la cena
f. estampillas
g. al ajedrez
h. un libro

Actividad C ¿Cierto o falso?

Indica si cada una de las siguientes oraciones es cierta o falsa.

		CIERTO	FALSO
1.	Meditar no es una actividad social, por lo general.	☐	☐
2.	Andar en bicicleta no es una actividad física.	☐	☐
3.	No es posible sacar un vídeo en la biblioteca.	☐	☐
4.	El ajedrez es un juego estratégico.	☐	☐
5.	Tocar el piano no es una actividad artística.	☐	☐
6.	Dar un paseo es una actividad sedentaria.	☐	☐
7.	Picar la comida es comer mucho.	☐	☐
8.	Bailar bien requiere mucha coordinación.	☐	☐

Go to page 123 to complete **¡Acción! 1.**

Gramática

Lo pasé muy bien.

**Preterite Tense of Regular
-ar Verbs**

Actividad D ¿Él o yo?

Listen to each sentence, then indicate if the verb used is in the **yo** or **él** form of the present or preterite tense. You will hear each sentence twice.

	YO: PRESENTE	ÉL: PRESENTE	YO: PRETÉRITO	ÉL: PRETÉRITO
1.	☐	☐	☐	☐
2.	☐	☐	☐	☐
3.	☐	☐	☐	☐
4.	☐	☐	☐	☐
5.	☐	☐	☐	☐
6.	☐	☐	☐	☐
7.	☐	☐	☐	☐
8.	☐	☐	☐	☐

Actividad E   ¿Quién?

Listen to each sentence. First, circle the subject of the sentence. Then indicate whether the written statement is a logical conclusion of what you heard (**lógico**) or not (**ilógico**). You will hear each sentence twice.

			LÓGICO	ILÓGICO
1.	**a.** yo **b.** tú **c.** un amigo	A la persona le gusta comer.	☐	☐
2.	**a.** yo **b.** tú **c.** un amigo	La persona es introvertida.	☐	☐
3.	**a.** nosotros **b.** otras personas	A las personas les gusta el arte.	☐	☐
4.	**a.** nosotros **b.** otras personas	A las personas no les gustan las actividades acuáticas.	☐	☐
5.	**a.** yo **b.** tú **c.** un amigo	La persona no está contenta con lo que hizo (*did*).	☐	☐
6.	**a.** yo **b.** tú **c.** un amigo	La persona desea ser artista.	☐	☐
7.	**a.** yo **b.** tú **c.** un amigo	Ahora la casa es de otro color.	☐	☐
8.	**a.** yo **b.** tú **c.** un amigo	La persona es introvertida.	☐	☐

Actividad F   ¿Yo u otra persona?

For each activity below, indicate whether the subject is **yo** or **otra persona**. For each statement that is about someone else, write the name of the famous person described.

		YO	OTRA PERSONA
1.	Pintó la *Mona Lisa*.	☐	☐ _____
2.	Estudié esta semana.	☐	☐ _____
3.	Navegó de España a América.	☐	☐ _____
4.	Hablé con un buen amigo.	☐	☐ _____
5.	Caminó en la luna.	☐	☐ _____
6.	Ayudó a Orville Wright.	☐	☐ _____

 Go to page 123 to complete ¡**Acción! 2.**

SEGUNDA PARTE

Vocabulario

El ejercicio y el gimnasio

Sports and Fitness

Actividad A Las actividades

Escucha las actividades y empareja cada una con la descripción correspondiente.

1. _____ Es como correr o trotar pero no tan rápido.

2. _____ En este deporte no se permite usar las manos. Requiere mucha agilidad.

3. _____ Es lo que hacen las personas que quieren fortalecer sus músculos.

4. _____ Esta actividad se hace en la nieve (*snow*) o sobre el agua.

5. _____ Para hacer esta actividad se necesita una bicicleta.

6. _____ Esta actividad se hace en el agua. Se necesita un traje de baño.

7. _____ Es un ejercicio aeróbico y es una buena manera de quemar calorías.

8. _____ Es lo que hace Tiger Woods como profesión.

Actividad B Los deportes

Indica la respuesta correcta.

1. Muchas personas juegan este deporte en un club privado.

   a. fútbol **b.** golf **c.** correr

2. Esta actividad se puede hacer en una piscina o en un lago (*lake*).

   a. caminar **b.** tenis **c.** nadar

3. Para esta actividad se necesitan una pelota (*ball*) y una red (*net*).

   a. vólibol **b.** nadar **c.** levantar pesas

4. Para llegar a ser (*To become*) «Mr. Universe», tienes que hacer esto.

   a. caminar **b.** levantar pesas **c.** nadar

5. Es como trotar, pero más rápido.

   a. caminar **b.** nadar **c.** correr

6. Puede ser estacionario o no.

   a. hacer ciclismo **b.** nadar **c.** levantar pesas

(continued)

7. En un juego entre dos personas, cuando una gana, ¿qué hace la otra?

    a. Suda.   **b.** Pierde.   **c.** Compite.

8. Puede ser aeróbico o no.

    a. ganar   **b.** hacer ejercicio   **c.** perder

Actividad C ¿Cierto o falso?

Indica si cada una de las siguientes oraciones es cierta o falsa.

		CIERTO	FALSO
1.	Tienes que ser muy joven para jugar al golf.	☐	☐
2.	Correr es una actividad aeróbica.	☐	☐
3.	Si compites, puedes ganar o puedes perder.	☐	☐
4.	Se puede nadar en la nieve.	☐	☐
5.	Si haces ejercicio aeróbico, vas a sudar.	☐	☐
6.	El vólibol es un deporte popular en la playa (*beach*).	☐	☐
7.	Esquiar puede ser una actividad acuática.	☐	☐
8.	Caminar no es una actividad acuática.	☐	☐

Go to page 123 to complete **¡Acción! 3.**

Gramática

Volví tarde.

**Preterite of Regular -er
and -ir Verbs**

Actividad D ¿Presente o pretérito?

Read each statement and indicate whether the verb is in the present or preterite tense.

		PRESENTE	PRETÉRITO
1.	Volvimos a tiempo.	☐	☐
2.	Conocimos al profesor.	☐	☐
3.	Hacemos el ciclismo.	☐	☐
4.	Perdimos el partido.	☐	☐
5.	Leemos mucho.	☐	☐
6.	Comimos tarde.	☐	☐
7.	Bebimos vino.	☐	☐
8.	No creemos eso.	☐	☐

Actividad E ¿A quién se refiere?

Listen to each statement and indicate to whom it refers. Pay attention to the verb endings. You will hear each statement twice.

1. _____
2. _____
3. _____
4. _____
5. _____
6. _____

    a. yo (*the speaker*)
    b. tú (*the listener*)
    c. tu compañero de clase
    d. mi familia y yo
    e. tú y tus compañeros (*in Spain*)
    f. tus hermanos

Actividad F ¿Quién?

Listen to each sentence. First, circle the subject of the sentence. Then indicate whether the written statement is a logical conclusion of what you heard (**lógico**) or not (**ilógico**). You will hear each sentence twice.

		LÓGICO	ILÓGICO
1. **a.** yo **b.** tú **c.** un amigo	La persona sudó.	☐	☐
2. **a.** yo **b.** tú **c.** un amigo	La persona quemó muchas calorías.	☐	☐
3. **a.** yo **b.** tú **c.** un amigo	La persona salió por la noche.	☐	☐
4. **a.** yo **b.** tú **c.** un amigo	La persona no sabe leer.	☐	☐
5. **a.** nosotros **b.** otras personas	No les gustan las bebidas alcohólicas.	☐	☐
6. **a.** nosotros **b.** otras personas	Otra persona enseñó algo.	☐	☐
7. **a.** yo **b.** tú **c.** un amigo	Ahora no puede pagar sus cuentas.	☐	☐
8. **a.** nosotros **b.** otras personas	El otro equipo ganó más puntos.	☐	☐

 Go to page 124 to complete ¡**Acción!** 4.

Vocabulario

¿Cuándo celebras tu cumpleaños? Special Occasions and Holidays

Actividad A Los días festivos

Escucha los nombres de los días festivos y empareja cada uno con la descripción correspondiente. Vas a oír cada día festivo dos veces.

1. _____ Es la última noche del año.

2. _____ Es una fiesta religiosa para los judíos. A veces coincide con la Navidad. Otro nombre para esta celebración es el Jánuka.

3. _____ Es un día para los románticos. También se llama el Día de los Enamorados.

4. _____ Es una fiesta religiosa para los cristianos que normalmente se celebra en abril.

5. _____ Es un día importante para los irlandeses. Se celebra en marzo y muchas personas llevan ropa verde.

6. _____ Es un día en el que se reúne la familia en los Estados Unidos. Todos comen mucho pavo y miran partidos de fútbol americano.

7. _____ A muchas personas les gusta ir a Nueva Orleáns o a Río de Janeiro para celebrar esta fiesta. Hay celebraciones tremendas.

8. _____ Es la noche antes de la Navidad.

Actividad B ¿Norte o sur?

Indica si las siguientes oraciones se refieren al hemisferio norte (N) o al hemisferio sur (S).

	N	S
1. Celebran la Navidad en verano.	☐	☐
2. Celebran la Pascua en la primavera.	☐	☐
3. Celebran el Martes de Carnaval en otoño.	☐	☐
4. Celebran la Nochebuena en invierno.	☐	☐
5. Celebran el Día de San Valentín en verano.	☐	☐
6. Celebran la Noche Vieja en verano.	☐	☐
7. Celebran el Día de Acción de Gracias en otoño.	☐	☐

Actividad C Asociaciones

Indica el concepto que *no* se asocia con el día festivo.

1. la Navidad

    a. los regalos   **b.** el color azul   **c.** una música especial

2. la Pascua

    a. la ropa nueva   **b.** los huevos   **c.** el color rojo

3. el Día de San Patricio

    a. los irlandeses (*Irish*)   **b.** el color verde   **c.** la ropa nueva

4. el Día de Acción de Gracias

    a. el pavo y el jamón **b.** los regalos   **c.** la familia

5. la Fiesta de las Luces

    a. el color verde   **b.** una música especial **c.** los regalos

6. la Noche Vieja

    a. el champán   **b.** el brindis   **c.** los dulces

 Go to page 124 to complete **¡Acción! 5.**

Gramática

¿Qué hiciste?   **Irregular Preterite Forms**

Actividad D ¿Él o yo?

Listen to each sentence, then indicate if the verb used is in the **yo** or **él** form of the present or preterite tense. You will hear each sentence twice.

	YO: PRESENTE	ÉL: PRESENTE	YO: PRETÉRITO	ÉL: PRETÉRITO
1.	☐	☐	☐	☐
2.	☐	☐	☐	☐
3.	☐	☐	☐	☐
4.	☐	☐	☐	☐
5.	☐	☐	☐	☐
6.	☐	☐	☐	☐
7.	☐	☐	☐	☐
8.	☐	☐	☐	☐

Actividad E En el tiempo libre

Match the correct verb to complete each sentence about the things different people did in their free time yesterday.

1. Yo _____ en bicicleta por dos horas.

2. Carlos _____ ejercicio aeróbico.

3. Nina y Javier _____ al teatro.

4. Anita y yo _____ un paseo.

5. Uds. _____ cinco vídeos de películas españolas a casa.

6, 7. Pedro _____ que tú no _____ nada.

8. Bárbara _____ en el gimnasio todo el día.

a. dimos
b. hizo
c. fueron
d. anduve
e. hiciste
f. estuvo
g. trajeron
h. dijo

Actividad F ¿Quién?

Listen to each sentence. First, circle the subject of the sentence. Then indicate whether the written statement is a logical conclusion of what you heard (**lógico**) or not (**ilógico**). You will hear each sentence twice.

			LÓGICO	ILÓGICO
1.	a. yo b. tú c. un amigo	Los amigos fueron también.	☐	☐
2.	a. yo b. tú c. un amigo	Ahora la persona lo siente (*regrets it*).	☐	☐
3.	a. yo b. tú c. un amigo	La persona es pragmática.	☐	☐
4.	a. nosotros b. otras personas	Todos los demás saben guardar (*to keep*) un secreto.	☐	☐
5.	a. yo b. tú c. un amigo	Al final la persona dijo algo.	☐	☐
6.	a. yo b. tú c. otra persona	La persona es padre.	☐	☐

Go to page 124 to complete ¡Acción! 6.

¡A escuchar!

Antes de escuchar

Paso 1 Escucha a Roberto y Marisela hablar del **Episodio 4.** Al principio de la conversación, Marisela le dice a Roberto que ella se considera (*considers herself*) una buena detective. ¿Qué crees que Marisela va a decir para mostrarle a (*show*) Roberto que es buena detective?

    ☐ que María es una mujer muy inteligente

    ☐ que descubrió (*she discovered*) algo

    ☐ que no le gustó Traimaqueo

Paso 2 Estudia las siguientes palabras y expresiones nuevas antes de escuchar la conversación.

la mentira	lie
mentir (i, i)*	to lie
el despistado	absent-minded guy
amable	nice
después de todo	after all
traer entre manos	to be up to something

A escuchar

Ahora escucha la conversación.

▲ Después de escuchar

Paso 1 Averigua tus respuestas para **Antes de escuchar, Paso 1.**

Paso 2 Ahora contesta las preguntas según la conversación entre Roberto y Marisela.

    1. Según Marisela, ¿quiénes son las dos personas que mintieron?

        ☐ Carlos y Traimaqueo

        ☐ Jaime y doña Isabel

        ☐ Carlos y Jaime

    2. Roberto piensa que doña Isabel…

        ☐ realmente está en Santiago.

        ☐ está loca.

        ☐ no está muy bien de salud.

(continued)

---

*The verb **mentir** has two stem-vowel changes in the preterite: **mintió** and **mintieron.** You will learn more about these stem changes in **Lección 4B.**

3. ¿Cómo justifica Roberto a Jaime?

    ☐ Dice que Jaime trata de ser cortés con María.

    ☐ Dice que Jaime trata de ser sincero con María.

    ☐ Dice que Jaime trata de ser un buen hombre de negocios.

4. Al final, Marisela sigue pensando que el viaje de Jaime a la viña Sol y viento fue malo.

    ☐ sí

    ☐ no

Estrategia

As you learned in your textbook, the preterite and the imperfect are two of the most frequently used verb forms to talk about the past in Spanish. The difference between them often expresses an idea that is not easily translated into English. It takes time to be able to use these verb forms correctly, but you can enhance your chances of acquiring them by paying close attention to their use in conversation. In this lesson, you are concentrating on the preterite. In most cases, an action has three phases: a beginning, a middle, and an end. The speaker will use the preterite when focusing on the beginning or the end of the action.

Paso 3 Escucha la conversación entre Roberto y Marisela otra vez. Primero, trata de identificar seis verbos en el pretérito y escríbelos en los espacios en blanco. Luego escribe el infinitivo de cada verbo en el segundo espacio en blanco. El primero ya está hecho (*is done*) para ti.

Ahora escucha la conversación.

	PRETÉRITO	INFINITIVO
1.	descubrí	descubrir
2.	_____	_____
3.	_____	_____
4.	_____	_____
5.	_____	_____
6.	_____	_____
7.	_____	_____

Paso 4 Roberto hace una pregunta al final de la conversación, pero Marisela no la contesta. Contesta la pregunta de Roberto en una o dos oraciones.

_____

_____

_____

_____

◉ 🎬 ¡Acción!

~~~~~~ ✳

¡Acción! 1   En los ratos libres

Escribe cinco oraciones sobre lo que te gusta hacer en tus ratos libres.

1. _____

2. _____

3. _____

4. _____

5. _____

¡Acción! 2   ¿Qué hiciste?

Contesta las siguientes preguntas sobre la última fiesta que asististe. Escribe oraciones completas.

1. ¿Lo pasaste muy bien?

_____

2. ¿Te rozaste con la gente?

_____

3. ¿Quiénes bailaron?

_____

4. ¿Sólo picaste la comida o comiste bien?

_____

5. ¿Tocaron música muy buena?

_____

¡Acción! 3   Los deportes

Escribe un párrafo de veinticinco a cincuenta palabras sobre los deportes que te gusta jugar, los deportes que te gusta observar y los deportes que no te gustan para nada (*at all*).

_____

_____

_____

_____

_____

_____

¡Acción! 4 Anoche

Usa los verbos de la lista para escribir oraciones que describen lo que las personas indicadas hicieron o no hicieron anoche.

aprender	comer	leer	ver
beber	correr	salir	volver

YO

1. _____

2. _____

EL PROFESOR (LA PROFESORA)

3. _____

4. _____

MIS COMPAÑEROS DE CLASE

5. _____

6. _____

¡Acción! 5 Los días festivos

Escribe cinco oraciones sobre cinco días festivos diferentes.

1. _____

2. _____

3. _____

4. _____

5. _____

¡Acción! 6 La semana pasada

Contesta las preguntas sobre la semana pasada. Escribe oraciones completas.

1. ¿Fuiste a algún lugar en especial? ¿Con quién?

_____

2. ¿Cuántas páginas del libro de español tuvieron Uds. que estudiar y/o preparar?

_____

3. ¿Hiciste preguntas en alguna clase?

_____

4. ¿Alguien dijo algo cómico en alguna clase?

_____

5. ¿Pudiste terminar todas las tareas antes de ir a clases?

_____

En casa

OBJETIVOS

IN THIS LESSON, YOU WILL CONTINUE TO PRACTICE:

- talking about dwellings and buildings

- talking about activities in the past tense with stem-changing -ir verbs in the preterite

- talking about rooms, furniture, and other items found in a house

- using reflexive pronouns to talk about what people do to and for themselves

- describing typical household chores

- identifying distinctions between **por** and **para**

Vocabulario

¿Dónde vives?   **Dwellings and Buildings**

 Actividad A   Descripciones

Escucha las palabras y frases y empareja cada una con la descripción correspondiente. Vas a oír cada palabra o frase dos veces.

1. _____ Es una persona que alquila un apartamento.

2. _____ Es un apartamento que se compra.

3. _____ Todos tus vecinos y tú viven allí.

4. _____ Si vives en un apartamento, puedes hacer una barbacoa allí.

5. _____ El edificio es de esta persona.

6. _____ Es el cuarto o el edificio donde trabaja una persona.

7. _____ Si vives aquí, probablemente eres estudiante.

8. _____ Si no compras tu casa, tienes que pagar esto cada mes.

Actividad B   ¿Cierto o falso?

Indica si cada una de las siguientes oraciones es cierta o falsa.

		CIERTO	FALSO
1.	El portero es la persona que comparte un cuarto contigo (*with you*).	☐	☐
2.	Las personas que viven en la misma zona son vecinos.	☐	☐
3.	Las viviendas con una vista buena son generalmente más caras.	☐	☐
4.	Las torres se encuentran en algunas iglesias y universidades.	☐	☐
5.	Antes de alquilar un piso, tienes que firmar un contrato.	☐	☐
6.	En España el piso es un apartamento.	☐	☐
7.	La dirección incluye el código postal (*zip code*).	☐	☐
8.	El hogar es un apartamento que alquilas, no es una casa.	☐	☐

Go to page 137 to complete **¡Acción! 1.**

Gramática

No durmió bien.　　　　　　**e → i, o → u Preterite Stem Changes**

Actividad C Presidentes de los Estados Unidos

Complete each description by matching it to the corresponding president(s).

1. _____ murió a los 46 años de edad, en 1963.

2. _____ fue electo a la presidencia por dos períodos consecutivos, de 1993 a 2001.

3. _____ y _____ murieron el mismo día (4 de julio de 1826).

4. _____ primero fue gobernador de Texas.

5. _____ murió asesinado en un teatro.

a. Lincoln
b. Adams
c. Bush
d. Jefferson
e. Clinton
f. Kennedy

Actividad D Los cuentos de hadas (*Fairy tales*)

Read the statements and match each one with the character it describes.

1. _____ Durmió durante cien años.

2. _____ Prefirió tener pies (*feet*) y no tener voz (*voice*).

3. _____ Murió al comer una manzana.

4. _____ El lobo (*wolf*) sintió hambre (*hungry*) cuando los vio.

5. _____ Le pidió al hada madrina (*fairy godmother*) un deseo.

6. _____ Divirtió a los ratones (*mice*) con su música.

7. _____ El lobo le sugirió un camino (*path*) largo.

a. la Cenicienta (*Cinderella*)
b. el flautista de Hamelín
c. Caperucita Roja (*Little Red Riding Hood*)
d. la Sirenita (*The Little Mermaid*)
e. la Bella Durmiente (*Sleeping Beauty*)
f. los tres cochinitos (*The Three Little Pigs*)
g. Blanca Nieves (*Snow White*)

Actividad E ¿Quién fue?

Listen to each statement, then indicate if the speaker is talking about what he and his roommate did or about what his friends did.

	MI COMPAÑERO Y YO	MIS AMIGOS
1.	☐	☐
2.	☐	☐
3.	☐	☐
4.	☐	☐
5.	☐	☐
6.	☐	☐
7.	☐	☐
8.	☐	☐

Go to page 137 to complete **¡Acción! 2.**

SEGUNDA PARTE

Vocabulario

Es mi sillón favorito.   **Furniture and Rooms**

Actividad A ¿Qué es?

Escucha las palabras y empareja cada una con la descripción correspondiente.

1. _____ Es el lugar donde ves la televisión con familia y amigos.

2. _____ Es el lugar donde pones la ropa cuando no la llevas.

3. _____ Es el lugar donde encuentras el lavabo y el inodoro.

4. _____ Es el lugar donde preparas la comida.

5. _____ Es el lugar donde encuentras el auto y las bicicletas de una familia.

6. _____ Es el lugar donde pones libros.

7. _____ Es el lugar donde duermes.

8. _____ Es el lugar donde sirves la comida.

Actividad B ¿Cierto o falso?

Indica si cada una de las siguientes oraciones es cierta o falsa.

		CIERTO	FALSO
1.	Es típico ver una bañera en la cocina.	☐	☐
2.	La ducha se encuentra en el jardín.	☐	☐
3.	Es bueno poner la lámpara donde uno lee más.	☐	☐
4.	En el patio típicamente se encuentran plantas.	☐	☐
5.	Un dormitorio amueblado no tiene armario ni cama.	☐	☐
6.	Una cama sencilla es más pequeña que una doble.	☐	☐
7.	Los cuadros van generalmente sobre la alfombra.	☐	☐
8.	Las mesitas se usan mucho en la sala.	☐	☐

 Go to page 138 to complete ¡Acción! 3.

Gramática

Me conozco bien.   **True Reflexive Constructions** ✳

Actividad C ¿Independiente o no?

Listen to each sentence and indicate whether it refers to something adults do to babies (**los bebés**) or to themselves (**los adultos**).

	LOS BEBÉS	LOS ADULTOS
1.	☐	☐
2.	☐	☐
3.	☐	☐
4.	☐	☐
5.	☐	☐
6.	☐	☐
7.	☐	☐
8.	☐	☐

Actividad D Problemas y soluciones

Match each problem with the most appropriate solution.

EL PROBLEMA

1. _____ Tienes que recordarte de una cita importante.

2. _____ Carlos Enrique se despierta tarde y tiene un examen en quince minutos.

3. _____ La hermanita de Roberto se distrae (*becomes distracted*) fácilmente;

4. _____ Paula ve a sus amigos en la cafetería.

5. _____ El hijo de Patty es pequeño y no sabe ponerse los zapatos bien.

6. _____ Tienes que recordarle a tu compañero de casa de pagar una cuenta.

LA SOLUCIÓN

a. Lo viste para la escuela.
b. Le escribes un mensaje.
c. Se viste para clase sin ducharse.
d. Se siente con ellos.
e. La siente en el comedor, donde no hay televisor, para hacer su tarea.
f. Te escribes un mensaje.

  Go to page 138 to complete **¡Acción! 4.**

TERCERA PARTE

Vocabulario

¿Te gusta lavar la ropa?   Domestic Chores and Routines

Actividad A Asociaciones

Empareja los verbos con los objetos correspondientes.

1. _____ lavar
2. _____ quitar
3. _____ pasar
4. _____ planchar
5. _____ barrer
6. _____ sacar
7. _____ poner en orden
8. _____ hacer

a. las cosas
b. el piso
c. la cama
d. los platos y la ropa
e. el polvo
f. la basura
g. la ropa
h. la aspiradora

Actividad B Los quehaceres domésticos

Escucha los quehaceres domésticos y empareja cada uno con la descripción correspondiente.

1. _____ Es pasar una escoba (*broom*).

2. _____ Es algo que hacemos con la ropa limpia y seca que todavía no se ve bien.

3. _____ Muchas personas hacen esto después de levantarse para arreglar un poco la habitación.

4. _____ Para hacer esto, es preferible usar un buen detergente y a veces es necesario usar lejía.

5. _____ Muchos hacen esto con jabón y una esponja (*sponge*) después de cada comida.

6. _____ Es limpiar la alfombra.

7. _____ Es poner todos los cuartos en orden.

8. _____ Es pasar el plumero (*feather duster*).

Actividad C ¿Qué se usa?

Indica la(s) palabra(s) correcta(s) para completar cada oración.

1. Para lavar los platos necesitas…
   a. lejía.
   b. jabón.
   c. aspiradora.

2. Para limpiar la alfombra utilizas…
   a. la aspiradora.
   b. la estufa.
   c. una plancha.

3. Quitas el polvo de…
   a. la secadora.
   b. la aspiradora.
   c. los muebles.

4. Limpias las ventanas con…
   a. toallas de papel.
   b. la lavadora.
   c. el refrigerador.

5. Al barrer, limpias…
   a. la cama.
   b. el piso.
   c. la ropa.

6. Después de lavar la ropa la pones en…
   a. el microondas.
   b. la secadora.
   c. el horno.

7. Pones el helado en...
   a. la nevera.
   b. la estufa.
   c. la plancha.

8. Lavas los platos en...
   a. el comedor.
   b. la sala.
   c. la cocina.

 Go to page 139 to complete ¡Acción! 5.

Gramática

¿Para mí?   Introduction to **por** Versus **para**

 Actividad D   ¿Por qué?

Listen to each sentence or question, then indicate the correct preposition to complete the response. You will hear each sentence or question twice.

1. ¿ _____ mí?

   ☐ Por

   ☐ Para

2. ¿ _____ cuándo?

   ☐ Por

   ☐ Para

3. _____ la mañana.

   ☐ Por

   ☐ Para

4. Vas a pasar _____ Madison, ¿no?

   ☐ por

   ☐ para

5. Sí, y sustituto la carne _____ el tofú.

   ☐ por

   ☐ para

6. Así que, lo hiciste _____ ella, ¿verdad?

   ☐ por

   ☐ para

Actividad E ¿Por o para?

Indicate the correct preposition to complete each sentence.

1. Mi hermano me fastidia (*annoys*) _____ placer (*pleasure*).

☐ por

☐ para

2. Voy _____ Miami mañana. Tengo familia allí.

☐ por

☐ para

3. Este contrato es _____ ti.

☐ por

☐ para

4. No hay vuelos (*flights*) directos. Tienes que pasar _____ Atlanta.

☐ por

☐ para

5. No tengo energía _____ la tarde.

☐ por

☐ para

6. Tengo que escribir la composición _____ el lunes.

☐ por

☐ para

7. Presté (*I gave*) servicio militar _____ mi país.

☐ por

☐ para

8. Esta tienda vende ropa _____ niños.

☐ por

☐ para

 Go to page 139 to complete **¡Acción! 6.**

 # Para escribir

Antes de escribir

Paso 1 Para esta actividad, vas a escribir una breve composición sobre los eventos más importantes en *Sol y viento* hasta el momento. Para comenzar, indica (✔) los eventos más importantes para narrar la historia. (Los espacios en blanco son para el **Paso 2.**)

_____ ☐ Jaime llegó a Santiago.

_____ ☐ Jaime conoció a María en el Parque Forestal.

_____ ☐ Mario se ofreció como chofer.

_____ ☐ Jaime llamó a Carlos.

_____ ☐ Jaime conoció a Carlos.

_____ ☐ Jaime conoció a Yolanda, la esposa de Traimaqueo.

_____ ☐ Jaime supo que Carlos le había mentido (*had lied to him*).

_____ ☐ Jaime salió a correr.

_____ ☐ Carlos le sirvió a Jaime una copa de un vino especial.

_____ ☐ Jaime dio con (*ran into*) María otra vez.

_____ ☐ Traimaqueo le dio a Jaime un tour de la bodega y la viña.

_____ ☐ Jaime invitó a María a tomar algo y ella aceptó.

Paso 2 Pon los eventos que marcaste en orden cronológico. Escribe los números en los espacios en blanco del **Paso 1.**

A escribir

Paso 1 Usa los eventos del **Paso 1** para escribir un borrador en una hoja de papel aparte. Las palabras y expresiones a continuación te pueden ser útiles.

al día siguiente	the next day
después	afterwards
después de + (*noun/infinitive*)	after + (*noun/infinitive*)
entonces	then
luego	then
más tarde	later
pero	but
y	and

Paso 2 Repasa bien lo que has escrito (*you have written*). ¿Quieres agregar (*to add*) oraciones para hacer la narración más interesante? Por ejemplo, en vez de decir: «Jaime fue al Parque Forestal para correr. Allí conoció a María», escribe algo como «Jaime fue a correr en el Parque Forestal donde conoció a María, una mujer joven, atractiva e inteligente».

Paso 3 Intercambia tu composición con la de un compañero (una compañera) de clase. Mientras lees su composición, revisa los siguientes puntos.

  ☐ el significado y el sentido en general

  ☐ la concordancia entre sustantivo y adjetivo

  ☐ la concordancia entre sujeto y verbo

  ☐ la ortografía

Al entregar la composición

Usa los comentarios de tu compañero/a de clase para escribir una versión final de tu composición. Repasa los siguientes puntos sobre el lenguaje y luego entrégale la composición a tu profesor(a).

  ☐ la concordancia entre sustantivos y adjetivos

  ☐ la forma correcta de verbos en el pretérito

 ¡Acción!

¡Acción! 1   En la universidad

Imagina que un amigo viene a estudiar en tu universidad. Escríbele una carta de veinticinco a cincuenta palabras para describir la vivienda aquí. ¿Qué opciones hay? ¿Es caro vivir aquí?

¡Hola, _____!:

_____

_____

_____

_____

_____

_____

_____

Un saludo,

_____ (tu nombre)

¡Acción! 2   ¿Buen compañero de cuarto?

Las siguientes oraciones describen lo que un compañero de cuarto hizo ayer. Primero, completa cada una con la forma correcta del verbo entre paréntesis. Luego, indica si te molesta lo que hizo o no. Cuando termines, indica si crees que Uds. podrían (*could*) ser buenos compañeros de cuarto o no.

	ME MOLESTA.	NO ME MOLESTA.
1. _____ (Dormir) hasta mediodía.	☐	☐
2. Le _____ (pedir) prestados (*he borrowed*) unos CDs a su compañero de cuarto.	☐	☐
3. Se _____ (servir) una porción de pizza que alguien dejó en el refrigerador.	☐	☐
4. Se _____ (divertir) hasta tarde con sus amigos.	☐	☐
5. Se _____ (sentir) ofendido cuando le dijeron que el apartamento no estaba limpio.	☐	☐
6. _____ (Conseguir) un gato como mascota.	☐	☐

Seríamos (*We would be*) buenos compañeros de cuarto.

☐ ¡Por cierto!

☐ Quizás. (*Perhaps.*)

☐ ¡Ni modo! (*No way!*)

¡Acción! 3 Mi casa

Contesta las siguientes preguntas sobre tu hogar. Escribe oraciones completas.

1. ¿Cuántos cuartos tiene?

   _____

2. Describe el exterior. ¿Tiene garaje? ¿patio? ¿jardín? ¿balcón?

   _____

3. ¿Cómo es tu habitación?

   _____

4. ¿Cómo es la cocina?

   _____

5. ¿Qué muebles y decoraciones hay?

   _____

¡Acción! 4 ¿Quién te conoce?

Paso 1 ¿Te conoces bien? Contesta las siguientes preguntas sobre tu comportamiento. Escribe oraciones completas.

1. ¿A qué actividades te dedicas?

   _____

2. ¿En qué situaciones te pones límites?

   _____

3. ¿En qué situaciones o con quién te expresas bien?

   _____

4. ¿En qué momentos te hablas a ti mismo/a?

   _____

5. ¿Cuándo y cómo te diviertes?

   _____

6. ¿Qué tipo de persona te imaginas que eres?

   _____

Paso 2 ¿Los demás te conocen bien? ¿Hay otra persona que podría (*could*) contestar las preguntas del **Paso 1** para ti? Contesta la pregunta a continuación.

   MODELOS: ¿Quiénes te conocen bien? →
   Nadie me conoce realmente. (Mis padres me conocen muy bien.)

   ¿Quiénes te conocen bien?

   _____

¡Acción! 5   ¿Tienes la casa limpia?

Contesta las siguientes preguntas sobre tu rutina de quehaceres domésticos. Escribe oraciones completas.

1. ¿Con qué frecuencia lavas los platos?

    _____

2. ¿Con qué frecuencia limpias el baño?

    _____

3. ¿Qué usas para quitar el polvo?

    _____

4. ¿Qué usas para lavar la ropa?

    _____

5. ¿Para qué usas toallas de papel?

    _____

¡Acción! 6   Personas famosas

Dé el nombre de una persona que hizo cada una de las siguientes cosas, y describe lo que pasó en una o dos oraciones. Trata de pensar en figuras históricas y políticas.

MODELO: alguien que hizo muchas cosas por el bienestar (*well-being*) de la sociedad →
          Benjamin Franklin hizo muchas cosas por el bienestar de la sociedad.
          Descubrió la electricidad, inventó los anteojos (*eyeglasses*) y fue uno de los
          fundadores (*founders*) de los Estados Unidos.

1. alguien que murió por su patria (*country*)

    _____

    _____

2. alguien que hizo algo bueno para mejorar la sociedad

    _____

    _____

3. alguien que viajó por un lugar (continente, país) muy poco conocido

    _____

    _____

4. alguien que fue elegido para una misión importante

    _____

    _____

La tecnología y yo

OBJETIVOS

IN THIS LESSON, YOU WILL CONTINUE TO PRACTICE:

- **words and expressions associated with computers and the Internet**

- **using verbs like gustar to talk about what interests you, bothers you, and so forth**

- **talking about useful electronic devices**

- **avoiding redundancy by using direct and indirect object pronouns together**

- **talking about your pastimes and activities now and when you were younger**

- **using imperfect verb forms to talk about what you used to do**

Vocabulario

Mi computadora

Computers and Computer Use

Actividad A **¿La computadora o la red?**

Indica si la palabra que oyes se asocia con la computadora o la red.

	LA COMPUTADORA	LA RED
1.	☐	☐
2.	☐	☐
3.	☐	☐
4.	☐	☐
5.	☐	☐
6.	☐	☐
7.	☐	☐
8.	☐	☐

Actividad B **Usando la computadora**

Pon en orden (del 1 al 8) las oraciones que describen algunas de las actividades típicas en la computadora. La primera está marcada.

_____ Se leen los mensajes nuevos.

_____ Se abre el programa del correo electrónico.

_____ Se hace clic en el botón «responder».

_____ Se conecta al Internet con el módem.

_____ Se escribe la contraseña para usar la computadora.

_____ Se apaga el programa del correo electrónico y la computadora.

___1___ Se enciende la computadora.

_____ Se escribe un mensaje y se le manda a la persona original.

Actividad C ¿Ventaja o desventaja? (*Advantage or disadvantage?*)

Las computadoras nos ofrecen muchas ventajas, pero presentan problemas también. Lee las oraciones e indica la respuesta más lógica. **¡OJO!** En algunos casos, hay más de una respuesta posible.

	VENTAJA	DESVENTAJA
1. Puedes estar en contacto con personas de todas partes del mundo.	☐	☐
2. Hay que guardar los documentos con frecuencia.	☐	☐
3. Las páginas Web contienen todo tipo de información.	☐	☐
4. Los disquetes son bastante frágiles.	☐	☐
5. Los estudiantes pueden hacer una búsqueda en la red en vez de tener que ir a la biblioteca.	☐	☐
6. Se puede descargar música.	☐	☐
7. A veces las computadoras se congelan.	☐	☐
8. El disco duro guarda muchísima información.	☐	☐

 Go to page 155 to complete **¡Acción! 1.**

Gramática

¡Me fascina!   Verbs like gustar

Actividad D Reacciones típicas

For each situation, select the response that makes the most sense.

1. Dos personas reciben una tarjeta electrónica el día de su aniversario.

   a. Les agrada.   **b.** No les importa.

2. Unos profesores descubren que sus estudiantes comparten por correo electrónico las respuestas para un examen.

   a. Les parece bien.   **b.** Les molesta mucho.

3. Los empleados de una compañía no pueden descargar documentos necesarios por correo electrónico.

   a. Les encanta.   **b.** No les gusta.

4. Dos secretarias reciben documentos electrónicos con virus destructivos.

   a. Les cae bastante bien.   **b.** Les cae muy mal.

5. Unos estudiantes intentan hacer una tarea en el Internet, pero el enlace no funciona.

   a. No les molesta.   **b.** Les molesta.

6. Los ejecutivos ocupados (*busy*) reciben el mismo mensaje de sus empleados diez veces.

   a. No les agrada.   **b.** Les encanta.

Actividad E ¿Afición o fobia?

Paso 1 Listen to each statement and indicate if the speaker is a computer fan (**Es aficionado/a**) or someone who is afraid of computers (**Tiene fobia**).

	ES AFICIONADO/A.	TIENE FOBIA.
1.	☐	☐
2.	☐	☐
3.	☐	☐
4.	☐	☐
5.	☐	☐
6.	☐	☐
7.	☐	☐
8.	☐	☐

Paso 2 Now listen to the statements from **Paso 1** again and indicate if you agree with the speaker (**A mí sí/también**) or not (**A mí no/tampoco**). Are you a fan of computers?

1. ☐ A mí también.

  ☐ A mí no.

2. ☐ A mí también.

  ☐ A mí no.

3. ☐ A mí sí.

  ☐ A mí tampoco.

4. ☐ A mí también.

  ☐ A mí no.

5. ☐ A mí también.

  ☐ A mí no.

6. ☐ A mí sí.

  ☐ A mí tampoco.

7. ☐ A mí también.

  ☐ A mí no.

8. ☐ A mí sí.

  ☐ A mí tampoco.

 Go to page 156 to complete **¡Acción! 2.**

SEGUNDA PARTE

Vocabulario

Mi celular

Electronic Devices

 Actividad A **Los aparatos electrónicos**

Paso 1 Indica si cada aparato electrónico que oyes es normalmente fijo o portátil.

	FIJO/A	PORTÁTIL
1.	☐	☐
2.	☐	☐
3.	☐	☐
4.	☐	☐
5.	☐	☐
6.	☐	☐
7.	☐	☐
8.	☐	☐

Paso 2 Ahora escucha la lista de aparatos del **Paso 1** otra vez y empareja cada uno con la palabra o frase correspondiente de la lista.

1. _____

2. _____

3. _____

4. _____

5. _____

6. _____

7. _____

8. _____

a. los números
b. los mensajes
c. las películas
d. las direcciones
e. los documentos urgentes
f. la música
g. las fotos
h. los mensajes de texto (*text messages*)

Actividad B Un mundo electrónico

Empareja las actividades y los accesorios con el aparato correspondiente. ¡OJO! Algunos se asocian con más de un aparato.

	EL TELEVISOR	EL TELÉFONO	EL ESTÉREO
1. el reproductor de CD	☐	☐	☐
2. el celular	☐	☐	☐
3. el juego electrónico	☐	☐	☐
4. el vídeo	☐	☐	☐
5. la máquina fax	☐	☐	☐
6. el mando a distancia	☐	☐	☐
7. hacer *zapping*	☐	☐	☐

Actividad C ¿Funciona o no?

Indica si el aparato descrito funciona o no.

	FUNCIONA.	NO FUNCIONA.
1. Enciendes la computadora y la pantalla te pide la contraseña.	☐	☐
2. En el estéreo se saltan (*skip*) algunas partes de las canciones.	☐	☐
3. La máquina fax no está conectada al teléfono.	☐	☐
4. Estás trabajando en la computadora y el programa se congela.	☐	☐
5. No puedes cambiar de canal con el mando a distancia.	☐	☐
6. Grabas un programa en la televisión con el reproductor de vídeo.	☐	☐
7. Marcas un número en el celular, pero ese número está comunicado (*busy*).	☐	☐
8. La calculadora te dice que dos más dos son cinco.	☐	☐

 Go to page 156 to complete ¡Acción! 3.

● Gramática

Ya te lo dije.   **Double-Object Pronouns**

Actividad D   ¿Me lo haces?

Listen to the questions and match each one to the correct response. You will hear each question twice.

1. ____
2. ____
3. ____
4. ____
5. ____
6. ____
7. ____
8. ____

a. Ya te las di.
b. Sí, sí. Se lo digo.
c. Ya te los devolví (*returned*).
d. Te la dejé en tu cuarto.
e. Creo que ya te lo di, ¿no?
f. No, ¿me la puedes explicar?
g. Sí, claro. ¿Me las puedes poner en el comedor?
h. Sí, ¿me lo puedes traer?

Actividad E   ¿Eres independiente o no?

Paso 1   Read each question, then circle the responses to each that are *not* grammatically possible.

1. ¿Te limpia la cocina otra persona?
   a. No, me la limpio yo.
   b. No, no me lo limpia.
   c. Sí, me la limpia.
   d. Sí, te la limpia.

2. ¿Te dicen tus padres: «Llámanos más»?
   a. No, no me lo dicen.
   b. No, no se lo dicen.
   c. Sí, me la dicen.
   d. Sí, me lo dicen.

3. ¿Te lava los platos otra persona?
   a. No, no me las lava.
   b. No, me los lavo yo.
   c. Sí, me los lava.
   d. Sí, se los lavo yo.

4. ¿Te da dinero otra persona?
   a. No, no me lo da.
   b. No, no se lo doy.
   c. Sí, me lo da.
   d. Sí, me la da.

(*continued*)

5. ¿Te paga las cuentas otra persona?
   a. No, no se las pago.
   b. No, me las pago yo.
   c. Sí, me las paga.
   d. Sí, me los paga.

Paso 2 Of the remaining answers for each item in **Paso 1,** write the letter of the one that describes your personal situation.

   1. _____   **2.** _____   **3.** _____   **4.** _____   **5.** _____

Paso 3 Use the following key to determine how independent you are.

   a or **b** = 1 point   **c** or **d** = 0 points

   (1.) _____ + (2.) _____ + (3.) _____ + (4.) _____ + (5.) _____ = _____

   5 = muy independiente   0 = muy consentido/a (*pampered*)

Actividad F ¿Se te aplica?

Indicate the most logical response for each situation.

1. Mis amigos me piden dinero, pero no lo tengo.

   a. No se lo doy.   **b.** No me lo dan.   **c.** Se lo doy.

2. Mi amigo tiene un problema, pero no quiere mis consejos.

   a. Me los pide igualmente.   **b.** No se los doy.   **c.** No me los da.

3. Tengo unos libros de texto que mi amigo necesita por un día y yo no los necesito.

   a. Me los da.   **b.** Se los doy.   **c.** Se lo doy.

4. Mi amiga olvidó (*forgot*) traer dinero en efectivo para su refresco y no aceptan tarjetas de crédito.

   a. Se lo pago.   **b.** Me la paga.   **c.** Me lo paga.

5. Una compañera me pide una goma de borrar (*eraser*) durante un examen.

   a. Me la pasa.   **b.** Se la doy.   **c.** Se lo doy.

6. Mi profesor hace una pregunta en clase y yo sé la respuesta.

   a. Me la contesta.   **b.** Se lo dice.   **c.** Se la contesto.

7. Encontré las monedas que perdió mi hermano.

   a. Me las da.   **b.** Se las doy.   **c.** Se lo doy.

Go to page 157 to complete ¡Acción! 4.

TERCERA PARTE

Vocabulario

Mi niñez y juventud

✱ Typical Childhood and Adolescent Activities

Actividad A ¿Cómo se portan?

Escucha las descripciones e indica si los niños se portan bien o mal.

	SE PORTAN BIEN.	SE PORTAN MAL.
1.	☐	☐
2.	☐	☐
3.	☐	☐
4.	☐	☐
5.	☐	☐
6.	☐	☐
7.	☐	☐
8.	☐	☐

Actividad B ¿Niños sedentarios (*inactive*)?

Indica si la actividad es sedentaria o activa.

		SEDENTARIA	ACTIVA
1.	jugar a los videojuegos	☐	☐
2.	pelearse con los hermanos	☐	☐
3.	subirse a los árboles	☐	☐
4.	colorear	☐	☐
5.	soñar con jugar al basquetbol	☐	☐
6.	leer las tiras cómicas	☐	☐
7.	jugar al escondite	☐	☐

Actividad C En los cuentos de hadas (*fairy tales*)

Indica el adjetivo que mejor describa al personaje.

1. Ricitos de Oro (*Goldilocks*) es…

    a. imaginativa.   **b.** traviesa.   **c.** adaptable.

2. Caperucita Roja (*Little Red Riding Hood*) no es…

    a. precavida.   **b.** impaciente.   **c.** torpe.

3. Pinocho es…

    a. obediente.   **b.** mentiroso.   **c.** cabezón.

4. La Cenicienta (*Cinderella*) es…

    a. torpe.   **b.** traviesa.   **c.** obediente.

5. Hansel y Gretel son…

    a. imaginativos.   **b.** enamorados.   **c.** traviesos.

6. Aladino es…

    a. travieso.   **b.** cabezón.   **c.** precavido.

 Go to page 158 to complete ¡**Acción!** 5.

Gramática

¿En qué trabajabas?

Introduction to the Imperfect Tense

Actividad D ¿Qué hacía?

An eighty-year-old man describes his childhood. Indicate if what he says is a lie (**mentira**) or if it's possibly true (**posible**).

		MENTIRA	POSIBLE
1.	Me burlaba de (*I made fun of*) las niñas para hacerlas llorar (*cry*).	☐	☐
2.	Hacía novillos con los maestros.	☐	☐
3.	Escribía la tarea en la computadora.	☐	☐
4.	Me encantaba jugar al escondite.	☐	☐
5.	Coloreaba encima de los cuadros de Picasso.	☐	☐
6.	Salía con Shakira.	☐	☐
7.	Hacía de (*I worked as*) niñero.	☐	☐
8.	Iba al cine con amigos.	☐	☐

Actividad E ¡Es mucho más fácil!

Match each electronic device with the problem or situation that it solves or changes.

Antes de comprarme…

1. _____ la agenda electrónica…

2. _____ la cámara digital…

3. _____ el contestador automático…

4. _____ los videojuegos…

5. _____ el mando a distancia…

6. _____ la máquina fax…

7. _____ la computadora…

8. _____ el teléfono celular…

a. me levantaba con frecuencia.
b. no recibía mensajes.
c. no recordaba las citas.
d. escribía a máquina (*on a typewriter*).
e. jugaba a las cartas.
f. usaba los teléfonos públicos.
g. gastaba mucho dinero en revelar las películas (*developing film*).
h. mandaba los documentos por correo.

Actividad F ¿Cómo era y cómo es hoy?

Listen to a woman describe what she was like and what she used to do as a child compared to now. Then indicate whether the statements below are true or false, based on what she says.

	CIERTO	FALSO
1. Era torpe.	☐	☐
2. Es físicamente activa.	☐	☐
3. Es sedentaria.	☐	☐
4. Era obediente.	☐	☐
5. Es imaginativa.	☐	☐
6. Usa muchos aparatos.	☐	☐
7. Es rebelde (*rebellious*).	☐	☐
8. Era traviesa.	☐	☐

 Go to page 157 to complete ¡Acción! 6.

¡A escuchar!

Antes de escuchar

Paso 1 Roberto y Marisela hablan del **Episodio 5.** ¿Qué crees que piensan de Carlos?

☐ Marisela tiene una opinión negativa de Carlos.

☐ Roberto tiene una opinión negativa de Carlos.

☐ Tanto Marisela como Roberto tiene una opinión negativa de Carlos.

☐ Tanto Marisela como Roberto tiene una opinión positiva de Carlos.

Paso 2 Estudia las siguientes palabras antes de escuchar la conversación entre Roberto y Marisela.

abrirse	to open up
encargarse	to be in charge
contratar	to hire
suficiente	enough
el resentimiento	resentment

A escuchar

Ahora escucha la conversación.

▲ Después de escuchar

Paso 1 Averigua tu respuesta para **Antes de escuchar, Paso 1,** en la clave de respuestas.

Paso 2 Contesta las siguientes preguntas basándote en la conversación entre Roberto y Marisela.

1. Roberto piensa que a María no le gusta Jaime.

☐ cierto

☐ falso

2. La actitud de Marisela hacia (*toward*) Jaime ha cambiado (*has changed*).

☐ cierto

☐ falso

3. Según Roberto, Carlos tuvo que encargarse de la viña porque…

☐ su madre se lo pidió.

☐ no había otra persona para hacer el trabajo.

☐ sus padres trabajaron mucho.

4. Roberto piensa que es buena idea contratar a un administrador.

☐ cierto

☐ falso

> **Estrategia**
>
> It is important to remember that understanding Spanish does not involve a word-for-word translation into English. In this lesson you have learned more about verbs like **gustar.** In contrast to English, the Spanish **gustar** construction is normally *verb + subject:* **Me** *caen* (*verb*) **mal** *las personas* (*subject*) **arrogantes.** Keeping this in mind will help you follow a conversation in Spanish when these verbs are used.

Paso 3 Escucha la conversación entre Roberto y Marisela otra vez, en la que usan verbos como **gustar** para expresar una reacción o una opinión de los personajes de *Sol y viento*. Mientras escuchas la conversación, completa las siguientes opiniones y observaciones de Roberto y Marisela sobre María, Jaime y Carlos.

> MODELO: a Marisela (la actitud de María) → A Marisela le encanta la actitud de María.

1. a Marisela (Jaime)

   _____

2. a Carlos (la viña)

   _____

3. a María y Jaime (saber más del otro)

   _____

4. a Marisela (Carlos)

   _____

5. a Carlos (su trabajo)

   _____

Paso 4 Ahora escribe tres o cuatro oraciones para explicar si estás de acuerdo con Roberto o con Marisela en cuanto al personaje de Carlos.

_____

_____

_____

_____

_____

_____

 ¡Acción!

¡Acción! 1 ¿Te ayuda? (*Does it help you?*)

Explica en una o dos oraciones si las siguientes actividades relacionadas con las computadoras te ayudan a aprender el español o no.

> MODELO: leer el periódico de un país hispanohablante →
> Leer el periódico me ayuda a aprender más vocabulario y a saber más de otro país.

1. descargar la música en español

   _____

   _____

2. comunicarme con los compañeros de la clase de español por correo electrónico

   _____

   _____

3. intercambiar mensajes en el Internet con alguien de un país de habla española

   _____

   _____

4. escribir mis tareas en un programa que tiene diccionario de español

   _____

   _____

5. buscar enlaces interesantes a las páginas Web en español

   _____

   _____

6. participar en una sala de chat en español

   _____

   _____

¡Acción! 2 ¿Qué te interesa en la red?

Usa las siguientes expresiones en dos oraciones completas para describir y explicar los tipos de página Web que te interesan o no.

encantar   gustar   interesar
fascinar   importar   molestar

MODELOS: las noticias →
Me importa saber lo que pasa en el mundo. Me gusta leer las noticias (*news*). (No me interesan las noticias. Me molesta leer cosas negativas.)

1. los deportes

_____

2. los pasatiempos (*hobbies*)

_____

3. los rompecabezas (*puzzles*) y otros juegos

_____

4. las compras

_____

5. las tiras cómicas y los chistes

_____

6. otro _____

_____

¡Acción! 3 ¿Ayuda o molesta?

Escribe una oración que describe cómo cada uno de los siguientes aparatos electrónicos pueden ser útiles o una molestia (*nuisance*).

MODELO: el estéreo →
Uno puede relajarse (*relax*) con la música del estéreo, pero el estéreo puede molestar cuando el volumen está demasiado alto.

1. el celular

_____

_____

2. el contestador automático

_____

_____

3. el mando a distancia

_____

_____

4. los juegos electrónicos

_____

_____

5. el televisor

_____

_____

6. la videocámara

_____

_____

¡Acción! 4 ¿Cómo son tus relaciones con tus amigos?

Paso 1 Contesta las siguientes preguntas sobre las relaciones entre tú y un buen amigo (una buena amiga). Usa oraciones completas.

1. ¿Te pide consejos (*advice*) tu amigo/a?

_____

2. ¿Le pides tú consejos a él/ella?

_____

3. ¿Te presta (*he/she lend*) dinero? ¿Le devuelves (*you return*) el dinero pronto (*soon*)?

_____

4. ¿Le prestas dinero tú a él/ella? ¿Te devuelve el dinero pronto?

_____

Paso 2 Basándote en tus respuestas a las preguntas del **Paso 1,** indica cuál de las declaraciones es cierta para tus relaciones con tu amigo/a.

☐ Somos generosos/as con los consejos.

☐ No somos generosos/as con los consejos.

☐ Somos generosos/as con el dinero.

☐ No somos generosos/as con el dinero.

¡Acción! 5 Las emociones de la niñez

Paso 1 Escribe una oración completa que describe las emociones que asocias o asociabas de niño/a con las siguientes frases. Explica por qué.

> MODELO: sacar la licencia de conducir →
> Sacar la licencia de conducir causa muchas tensiones porque es muy importante, pero también muy difícil.

1. leer las tiras cómicas

_____

_____

2. enamorarse

_____

_____

3. pelearse con otros niños

_____

_____

4. comerse las uñas

_____

_____

5. colorear

_____

_____

Paso 2 En general, ¿con qué emociones asocias tu niñez?

_____

_____

¡Acción! 6 De niño/a

Habla con un pariente o amigo/a mayor que tú y hazle preguntas sobre lo que él/ella hacía de niño/a. Luego, escribe un párrafo de veinticinco a cincuenta palabras para describir la niñez y juventud de esa persona. (Si prefieres, puedes describir tu propia [*your own*] niñez o juventud.)

_____

_____

_____

_____

_____

Érase una vez...

OBJETIVOS

**IN THIS LESSON,
YOU WILL
CONTINUE TO
PRACTICE:**

- **expressing years,
  decades, and
  centuries**

- **using the preterite
  and the imperfect
  together to
  narrate events**

- **talking about
  important
  historical events**

- **talking about
  important
  personal events**

Vocabulario

En 1972...   **Numbers 1,000 and Higher**

Actividad A   ¿En qué orden?

Apunta los números que oyes y luego ponlos en orden, del menor al mayor. Vas a oír cada número dos veces.

	NÚMERO	ORDEN
1.	_____	_____
2.	_____	_____
3.	_____	_____
4.	_____	_____
5.	_____	_____
6.	_____	_____
7.	_____	_____
8.	_____	_____

Actividad B   ¿En qué siglo?

Primero, escribe cada año en números. Luego, empareja el año con el siglo correspondiente. El primero ya está hecho (*is done*) para ti.

1. __b__ mil ochocientos setenta y tres: ___1873___

2. ____ mil diez: _____

3. ____ mil seiscientos veintitrés: _____

4. ____ mil doscientos ochenta y seis: _____

5. ____ mil trescientos doce: _____

6. ____ dos mil cincuenta y dos: _____

7. ____ mil cuatrocientos noventa y dos: _____

8. ____ mil setecientos setenta y seis: _____

a. XIII (trece)
b. XIX (diecinueve)
c. XXI (veintiuno)
d. XVIII (dieciocho)
e. XV (quince)
f. XI (once)
g. XIV (catorce)
h. XVII (diecisiete)

Go to page 169 to complete **¡Acción! 1.**

● Gramática

¿Qué hacías cuando te llamé?

Contrasting the Preterite and Imperfect

Actividad C ¿Quién pregunta?

Match each person with an appropriate question.

1. _____ el detective
2. _____ el instructor
3. _____ el policía
4. _____ el médico (*doctor*)
5. _____ el jefe (*boss*)
6. _____ el novio

a. ¿Cómo te sentías cuando decidiste tomar esa medicina?
b. ¿Dónde estabas cuando sonó la campana (*the bell rang*)?
c. ¿En qué pensaba Ud. cuando escribió este informe (*report*)?
d. ¿Dónde estabas anoche cuando te llamé?
e. ¿Qué dijo el hombre mientras sacaba el revólver?
f. ¿Sabe Ud. a qué velocidad (*speed*) iba cuando me pasó?

○ **Actividad D** ¿Qué pasó?

Circle the best option to finish each sentence that you hear. You will hear each sentence twice.

1. a. cuando tomé el examen.
    b. el día que me gradué.
    c. cuando vi el accidente.

2. a. cuando conocí a mi novia.
    b. cuando fui al gimnasio.
    c. cuando asistí a mi primera clase de español.

3. a. cuando me gradué de la universidad.
    b. cuando entré en la escuela primaria (*elementary*).
    c. cuando saqué la licencia de conducir.

4. a. cuando supe (*I found out*) de la guerra (*war*).
    b. cuando terminé el examen.
    c. cuando llegué al aeropuerto.

5. a. cuando me dormí.
    b. cuando me acosté.
    c. cuando me despertó el teléfono.

6. a. cuando me senté a tomar un café.
    b. cuando recordé que tenía un examen.
    c. cuando perdí el avión.

Actividad E ¿Dónde estaba?

Match the phrase that would logically complete each sentence.

1. _____ La madre todavía preparaba la cena cuando…

2. _____ Los estudiantes todavía hacían sus exámenes cuando…

3. _____ Antonio todavía levantaba pesas cuando…

4. _____ Laura no oyó el teléfono porque…

5. _____ El ladrón (*thief*) entró y salió con las joyas (*jewelry*) mientras…

6. _____ El equipo perdió el partido que…

7. _____ José Luis quitó la mesa mientras…

8. _____ Los niños veían su programa de televisión favorito cuando…

a. todavía pasaba la aspiradora.
b. se apagaron las luces y el televisor.
c. tenía que ganar para entrar en el campeonato.
d. la familia tomaba el postre y un café en la sala.
e. el profesor dijo que ya era hora de entregárselos.
f. cerraron el gimnasio.
g. los hijos llegaron a casa para comer.
h. el perro dormía sin oír nada.

 Go to page 169 to complete ¡**Acción!** 2.

Go to page 169 to complete ¡**Acción!** 2.

SEGUNDA PARTE

Vocabulario

Durante la guerra…   **Important Events and Occurrences**

Actividad A ¡Busca el intruso!

Indica la palabra que *no* se asocia con la primera palabra.

1. la guerra

   a. la revolución   b. invadir   c. el terremoto

2. las inundaciones

   a. la lluvia (*rain*)   b. la invasión   c. el agua

3. el huracán

   a. el terremoto   b. la lluvia   c. el viento

4. la depresión económica

   a. el dinero   b. las fiestas   c. la pobreza (*poverty*)

5. la exploración

   a. descubrir **b.** la llegada **c.** la revolución

6. la independencia

   a. celebrar **b.** la revolución **c.** el descubrimiento

 Actividad B Asociaciones

Escucha cada palabra o frase e indica las palabras o expresiones correspondientes.

1. _____	**a.** la falla (*fault*) de San Andreas
	b. los pasaportes
2. _____	**c.** el espacio y el sistema solar
3. _____	**d.** la Bolsa de valores (*stock market*)
	e. Katrina, Andrew, Mitch
4. _____	**f.** 1776
	g. civil
5. _____	**h.** el río (*river*) Misisipí, el río Nilo
6. _____	
7. _____	
8. _____	

Actividad C Y todo cambió

Lee cada oración y emparéjala con el evento correspondiente.

1. _____ El presidente caminaba con su guardaespaldas (*bodyguard*) cuando un hombre le disparó (*shot*).

2. _____ Todo iba muy bien cuando los precios subieron hasta el cielo (*climbed sky-high*).

3. _____ La gente dormía cuando todo empezó a temblar (*tremble*).

4. _____ El primer ministro se reunía con unos senadores cuando entraron los militares y tomaron el poder (*power*).

5. _____ El cacique (*chief*) indígena reinaba (*ruled*) sobre su gente cuando llegaron los europeos e impusieron (*imposed*) un nuevo régimen.

6. _____ El cielo se puso (*became*) negro, empezó a llover muchísimo y un viento muy fuerte destruyó (*destroyed*) los árboles.

7. _____ La gente que vivía en la colonia decidió luchar (*to fight*) por su independencia.

a. un golpe de estado (*military coup*)
b. un terremoto
c. una revolución
d. un asesinato (*assassination*)
e. una conquista
f. un huracán
g. una crisis económica

 Go to page 170 to complete **¡Acción! 3.**

Gramática

Actividad D ¿Qué pasó?

Indicate if the sentences you hear describe actions that have been completed (**realizada**), not completed (**no realizada**), or if it is unknown whether the action was completed or not (**No se sabe**).

	REALIZADA	NO REALIZADA	NO SE SABE
1.	☐	☐	☐
2.	☐	☐	☐
3.	☐	☐	☐
4.	☐	☐	☐
5.	☐	☐	☐
6.	☐	☐	☐
7.	☐	☐	☐
8.	☐	☐	☐

Actividad E Ya lo conocía

Select the option that best completes each statement.

1. Anoche me presentaron (*they introduced*) a Jason. Así es como…

   a. lo conocía. **b.** lo conocí.

2. Fue Cristina quien le dijo a Marisela que Alicia y David se separaron. Hasta ese momento, Marisela…

   a. no lo sabía. **b.** no lo supo.

3. Te llamamos varias veces pero no contestaste. Así que…

   a. no podíamos conseguirte. **b.** no pudimos conseguirte.

4. José era muy buen amigo mío. Así que ya…

   a. lo conocía bastante bien. **b.** lo conocí en la fiesta.

5. Sergio estudió y enseñó filosofía durante muchos años. Me imagino que…

   a. sabía algo de Aristóteles. **b.** supo algo de Aristóteles.

6. Tomé un curso de tejer (*weaving*) porque…

   a. quería aprender algo nuevo. **b.** quise aprender algo nuevo.

Actividad F Claudia

Listen to what Claudia (a university student) says, then indicate the corresponding sentence. You will hear each of Claudia's statements twice.

1. ☐ Claudia no quería trabajar con David.

    ☐ Claudia no quiso trabajar con David.

2. ☐ Lo conocía bien.

    ☐ Lo conoció hace poco tiempo.

3. ☐ Ya sabía del divorcio de Javier.

    ☐ Supo del divorcio de Javier.

4. ☐ Pudo terminarlo.

    ☐ Podía terminarlo.

5. ☐ Quería ir al cine.

    ☐ Quiso ir al cine.

6. ☐ Conoció Buenos Aires en ese viaje.

    ☐ Ya conocía Buenos Aires.

 Go to page 170 to complete ¡Acción! 4.

TERCERA PARTE

Vocabulario

Me gradué en 2000.

Personal Events, Triumphs, and Failures

Actividad A Los eventos importantes

Lee cada oración y emparéjala con el evento correspondiente.

1. _____ Les compré una cafetera y toallas de cocina.
2. _____ Les compré ropa de bebé.
3. _____ Le envié una tarjeta de simpatía.
4. _____ Les regalé un adorno (_decoration_) para la casa nueva.
5. _____ La invité a cenar para conocer a gente nueva.
6. _____ Le compramos una pluma elegante y un reloj.

a. la muerte del esposo de Luisa
b. la graduación de Marcos
c. el nacimiento del primer hijo de Carla y Ramón
d. el divorcio de Rosa
e. la boda de Ángela y Pedro
f. la mudanza de Olga y Andrés

Actividad B   Opuestos

Escucha cada palabra y emparéjala con la palabra opuesta.

1. _____
2. _____
3. _____
4. _____
5. _____
6. _____
7. _____
8. _____

    a. morir
    b. quedarse
    c. tumultuoso
    d. divorciarse
    e. perder
    f. alegre
    g. fracasar
    h. pasarlo mal

Go to page 171 to complete ¡Acción! 5.

Gramática

Tenía 30 años cuando nació mi primer hijo.

Summary of the Preterite and Imperfect

Actividad C   ¿Te interrumpen?

Indicate whether the interrupting action in each sentence is a help (**ayuda**) or a distraction (**distracción**).

	AYUDA	DISTRACCIÓN
1. **Escribías** un trabajo (*paper*) cuando tu compañero/a de cuarto encendió la televisión.	☐	☐
2. Un joven **conducía** cuando recibió una llamada en el celular.	☐	☐
3. Un estudiante **trabajaba** en la computadora cuando el programa corrigió (*corrected*) la gramática en su última oración.	☐	☐
4. Un joven **conducía** cuando vio que el semáforo (*traffic light*) cambiaba a rojo.	☐	☐
5. Un estudiante **escribía** en la computadora cuando se abrió un anuncio «*pop-up*» en la pantalla.	☐	☐
6. **Escribías** un trabajo cuando se te ocurrió una buena conclusión.	☐	☐
7. **Hacías** tus planes de boda cuando recibiste un regalo de mil dólares de tus tíos.	☐	☐
8. **Trabajabas** en un proyecto importante cuando tu amigo te llamó para charlar de sus vacaciones.	☐	☐

Actividad D ¿Qué pasó?

Match each situation that you hear with the corresponding event.

1. _____
2. _____
3. _____
4. _____
5. _____
6. _____

    a. la muerte
    b. el cumpleaños
    c. la mudanza
    d. la boda
    e. el nacimiento
    f. la graduación

Go to page 171 to complete **¡Acción! 6.**

✎ Para escribir

Antes de escribir

Paso 1 Para esta actividad, vas a escribir una breve narración sobre los eventos del día perfecto desde el punto de vista (*point of view*) de María o Jaime. Para comenzar, indica quién de los dos diría (*would say*) las siguientes oraciones. **¡OJO!** En algunos casos puede ser los dos. (Los espacios en blanco son para el **Paso 2.**)

		JAIME	MARÍA
1.	_____ La esperaba (*I waited*) en la entrada (*entrance*) del funicular.	☐	☐
2.	_____ Leía un artículo con mi foto cuando llegué.	☐	☐
3.	_____ ¡Me besó (*kissed*)!	☐	☐
4.	_____ Se me olvidó (*I forgot*) por completo mi cita con Diego.	☐	☐
5.	_____ Pensé que tenía otro novio (*boyfriend*).	☐	☐
6.	_____ Tomamos una copa de vino y hablamos un poco de mi familia.	☐	☐
7.	_____ Lo pasábamos muy bien cuando llamó Diego.	☐	☐
8.	_____ Tuvo que salir.	☐	☐
9.	_____ Fue un día perfecto.	☐	☐
10.	_____ Su trabajo me parecía muy interesante.	☐	☐
11.	_____ Mientras subíamos en el funicular hablábamos de su trabajo y del mío.	☐	☐

Paso 2 Ahora decide si vas a narrar los eventos del día desde la perspectiva de Jaime o María y pon los eventos del **Paso 1** en orden cronológico. Escribe los números en los espacios en blanco del **Paso 1.**

(*continued*)

A escribir

Paso 1 Usa los eventos del **Paso 1** de **Antes de escribir** para escribir un borrador en una hoja de papel aparte. Puedes utilizar las oraciones del personaje que *no* eligiste para dar más información, pero recuerda que vas a tener que cambiar algunos pronombres y verbos. Las palabras y expresiones a continuación te pueden ser útiles.

de repente	suddenly
desafortunadamente	unfortunately
después	afterwards
después de + (*noun/infinitive*)	after + (*noun/infinitive*)
entonces	then
luego	then
más tarde	later
pero	but
por fin	finally
y	and

Paso 2 Repasa bien lo que has escrito. ¿Quieres agregar (*to add*) palabras, expresiones u oraciones para hacer la narración más interesante?

Paso 3 Intercambia tu composición con la de un compañero (una compañera) de clase. Mientras lees su composición, revisa los siguientes puntos.

☐ el significado y el sentido en general

☐ la concordancia entre sustantivo y adjetivo

☐ la concordancia entre sujeto y verbo

☐ la ortografía

Al entregar la composición

Usa los comentarios de tu compañero/a de clase para escribir una versión final de tu composición. Repasa los siguientes puntos sobre el lenguaje y luego entrega la composición a tu profesor(a).

☐ el uso del pretérito y del imperfecto

☐ la forma correcta de los pronombres

 **¡Acción!**

¡Acción! 1 ¿Cuántos hay?

Contesta cada pregunta con una oración completa. Escribe el número correcto en palabras.

> MODELO: ¿Cuántos minutos hay en veinticuatro horas? → Hay mil cuatrocientos cuarenta minutos en veinticuatro horas.

1. ¿Cuántos segundos hay en una hora?

   _____

2. ¿Cuántas pulgadas (*inches*) hay en doscientos pies (*feet*)?

   _____

3. ¿Cuántos años hay en un milenio?

   _____

4. ¿Cuántos minutos hay en una semana?

   _____

5. ¿Cuántos milímetros hay en dos metros y medio?

   _____

6. ¿Cuántos huevos hay en dos mil docenas (*dozen*)?

   _____

¡Acción! 2 ¿Le puedo hacer una pregunta?

Escribe preguntas para seis personas históricas para saber qué pasaba cuando hicieron algo importante.

> MODELO: Colón → ¿Adónde iba Ud. cuando llegó a América?

1. _____
2. _____
3. _____
4. _____
5. _____
6. _____

¡Acción! 3 La época actual (*current*)

En tu opinión, ¿qué eventos actuales puedes describir con los siguientes adjetivos? Escribe una oración completa con el adjetivo dado (*given*).

    MODELO: difícil → Es una época difícil por los problemas del medioambiente.

1. emocionante

    _____

2. estable

    _____

3. feliz

    _____

4. oscuro

    _____

5. pacífico

    _____

6. tumultuoso

    _____

¡Acción! 4 En esta clase

Contesta las siguientes preguntas sobre tu clase de español. Escribe oraciones completas.

    MODELO: ¿A quién(es) conocías en esta clase? → Yo no conocía a nadie.

1. ¿Cómo conociste al profesor (a la profesora)?

    _____

2. ¿Qué sabías de este curso antes de tomarlo?

    _____

3. ¿Cuánto español sabías antes de este curso?

    _____

4. ¿Qué supiste de este curso el primer día?

    _____

5. ¿Hay algo que no sabías decir en español pero que ahora sí sabes cómo decirlo?

    _____

6. ¿Hay algo que no hiciste para esta clase?

    _____

¡Acción! 5   Una definición personal

Escribe un párrafo de veinticinco a cincuenta palabras para definir lo que es tener éxito en tu vida personal.

_____

_____

_____

_____

_____

¡Acción! 6   El fracaso

Contesta las siguientes preguntas. Escribe oraciones completas.

1. ¿Hay algo que intentaste hacer alguna vez pero que no conseguiste hacer?

   _____

2. ¿Cuántos años tenías cuando ocurrió?

   _____

3. ¿Cómo te sentías al fracasar?

   _____

4. ¿Qué dijeron los demás?

   _____

5. ¿Qué hiciste para recuperarte de ese fracaso?

   _____

6. ¿Aprendiste algo de la experiencia?

   _____

Answer Key

Lección preliminar

PRIMERA PARTE

Vocabulario

Actividad A 3, 5, 4, 2, 1

Gramática

Actividad C **1.** Guatemala **2.** Italia **3.** Rusia **4.** Cuba **5.** Francia **6.** Ecuador **7.** España **8.** Venezuela **Actividad E** **1.** b **2.** c **3.** b **4.** d **5.** a **6.** d

SEGUNDA PARTE

Vocabulario

Actividad A **1.** b **2.** c **3.** a **4.** b **5.** b **6.** a **7.** b **8.** a **Actividad C** **1.** e **2.** g **3.** b **4.** h **5.** d **6.** a **7.** c **8.** f

Gramática

Actividad E **1.** b (no) **2.** d (no) **3.** a (sí) **4.** b (no) **5.** a (sí) **6.** a (no) **7.** d (sí) **8.** c (sí)

TERCERA PARTE

Vocabulario

Actividad B **1.** cierto **2.** falso **3.** cierto **4.** cierto **5.** cierto **6.** falso

Gramática

Actividad C **1.** b **2.** a **3.** b **4.** b **5.** a **6.** c **7.** b **8.** a

Lección 1A

PRIMERA PARTE

Vocabulario

Actividad A **1.** 793-4106 **2.** 549-4331 **3.** 879-3132 **4.** 996-4131 **5.** 931-3486 **6.** 286-0294 **7.** 631-7254 **8.** 403-8679 **Actividad B** **1.** 16 + 6 = 22 **2.** 30 − 13 = 17 **3.** 4 + 11 = 15 **4.** 3 + 25 = 28 **5.** 8 − 2 = 6 **6.** 10 + 20 = 30 **7.** 14 − 5 = 9 **8.** 15 − 2 = 13 **Actividad C** **1.** falso **2.** cierto **3.** falso **4.** cierto **5.** falso **6.** falso **7.** cierto **8.** falso

Gramática

Actividad E **1.** f **2.** c **3.** a **4.** e **5.** h **6.** d **7.** g **8.** b

SEGUNDA PARTE

Vocabulario

Actividad B **1.** b **2.** a **3.** a **4.** c **5.** b **6.** b

Gramática

Actividad E 1. d 2. c 3. b 4. e 5. a 6. g 7. h 8. f **Actividad F** 1. c 2. c 3. c 4. a 5. a 6. b 7. a 8. b

TERCERA PARTE

Vocabulario

Actividad B 1. b 2. a 3. b 4. b 5. a 6. b 7. a 8. a **Actividad C** 1. b 2. a 3. c 4. b 5. b 6. a

Gramática

Actividad D 1. b 2. b 3. a 4. c 5. a 6. c

¡A escuchar!

Después de escuchar
Paso 1 They offer opinions about what happened. **Paso 2** 1. no 2. sí 3. Cree que tiene un secreto.
Paso 3 (*Order may vary.*) 1. servil 2. posiblemente 3. expresión 4. siniestra 5. preocupación

Lección 1B

PRIMERA PARTE

Vocabulario

Actividad B 1. unas chicas 2. la informática 3. en la biblioteca 4. los lunes y miércoles 5. a mi amigo 6. en la sala de clase 7. una película mexicana 8. Necesito comprar un libro. **Actividad C** 1. a 2. b 3. e 4. f 5. d 6. c

Gramática

Actividad E 1. c 2. e 3. f 4. a 5. g 6. h 7. b 8. d

SEGUNDA PARTE

Vocabulario

Actividad C **Paso 1** 1. S 2. N 3. N 4. S 5. N 6. S 7. N 8. S **Paso 2** 1. invierno 2. invierno 3. invierno 4. verano 5. verano 6. invierno 7. invierno 8. verano

Gramática

Actividad E 1. d 2. b 3. f 4. c 5. a 6. e

TERCERA PARTE

Vocabulario

Actividad B 1. e 2. c 3. f 4. a 5. b 6. d **Actividad C** 1. c 2. a 3. g 4. b 5. f 6. h 7. e 8. d

Gramática

Actividad E 1. a 2. b 3. a 4. a 5. b 6. b 7. a 8. a

Lección 2A

Vocabulario

Actividad A **1.** 71 **2.** 42 **3.** 93 **4.** 68 **5.** 55 **6.** 39 **7.** 80 **8.** 100 **Actividad B** **Paso 1** **1.** Leticia (36), Nancy (28); Leticia **2.** Sergio (16), Marcela (21); Marcela **3.** Rosa María (42), Marcos (43); Marcos **4.** Rodrigo (84), Leonora (59); Rodrigo **5.** Alba (70), Gabriela (63); Alba **6.** Pablo (15), Andrés (33); Andrés **Paso 2** Rodrigo es el mayor de todos. **Actividad C** **1.** adulto **2.** adolescente **3.** adulto **4.** anciano **5.** adolescente **6.** anciano **7.** adulto **8.** anciano

Gramática

Actividad E **Paso 1** **1.** no **2.** sí **3.** no **4.** no **5.** sí **6.** sí

Vocabulario

Actividad B **1.** una universidad hispana **2.** una universidad norteamericana **3.** una universidad hispana **4.** una universidad norteamericana **5.** una universidad norteamericana **6.** una universidad norteamericana **Actividad C** **1.** no **2.** no **3.** sí **4.** sí **5.** no **6.** sí **7.** no **8.** no

Gramática

Actividad E **1.** e **2.** f **3.** c **4.** a **5.** d **6.** b

Vocabulario

Actividad A **1.** c **2.** a **3.** c **4.** b **5.** a **6.** b **7.** c **Actividad C** **1.** e **2.** g **3.** d **4.** h **5.** f **6.** a **7.** b **8.** c

Gramática

Actividad D **1.** por la tarde **2.** por la noche **3.** por la noche **4.** por la mañana **5.** por la tarde/noche **6.** por la mañana **7.** por la tarde/noche **Actividad F** **1.** sí **2.** sí **3.** no **4.** no **5.** no **6.** sí

¡A escuchar!

Después de escuchar
Paso 1 Roberto and Marisela talk about Jaime and María.
Paso 2 **1.** sí **2.** no **3.** 30 **4.** Piensa que Jaime es una persona privada. **Paso 3** **2.** pienso, pensar, e → ie **3.** tienen, tener, e → ie **4.** miente, mentir, e → ie **5.** recuerdo, recordar, o → ue **6.** piensas, pensar, e → ie **7.** quiere, querer, e → ie

Lección 2B

Vocabulario

Actividad B **1.** c **2.** d **3.** d **4.** b **5.** a **6.** c **7.** b **8.** a **Actividad C** **1.** b **2.** a **3.** a **4.** b **5.** a **6.** a

Gramática

Actividad E **1.** d **2.** e **3.** b **4.** g **5.** f **6.** c **7.** a

SEGUNDA PARTE

Vocabulario

Actividad C **1.** d **2.** g **3.** b **4.** f **5.** h **6.** e **7.** a **8.** c

Gramática

Actividad E **1.** b **2.** c **3.** a **4.** c **5.** a **6.** d

TERCERA PARTE

Vocabulario

Actividad A 5, 3, 7, 6, 1, 8, 9, 2, 4 **Actividad C** **1.** d **2.** e **3.** a **4.** f **5.** b **6.** c

Gramática

Actividad D **Paso 2** Normalmente Eduardo es una persona divertida, pero hoy está de mal humor.
Actividad E **1.** descripción **2.** cambio **3.** cambio **4.** descripción **5.** cambio **6.** cambio
Actividad F **1.** Es **2.** es **3.** Está **4.** Es **5.** es **6.** está **7.** Está **8.** está

Lección 3A

PRIMERA PARTE

Vocabulario

Actividad B **1.** b **2.** a **3.** c **4.** b **5.** c **6.** a **Actividad C** **1.** b **2.** c **3.** c **4.** a **5.** a **6.** b

Gramática

Actividad D **1.** Sabes **2.** Conoces **3.** Conoces **4.** Conoces **5.** Sabes **6.** Conoces **Actividad E**
1. David Letterman conoce la ciudad de Nueva York. (lógico) **2.** Shania Twain sabe jugar al fútbol.
(ilógico) **3.** Celene Dion sabe hablar chino. (ilógico) **4.** Einstein sabe mucho de física. (lógico)
5. Madonna sabe cantar. (lógico) **6.** George W. Bush sabe hablar muchos idiomas. (ilógico) **7.** Salma
Hayek conoce a Antonio Banderas. (lógico) **8.** Carlos Santana sabe tocar la trompeta. (ilógico)
Actividad F **1.** a **2.** a **3.** b **4.** b **5.** b **6.** a

SEGUNDA PARTE

Vocabulario

Actividad A **1.** c **2.** b **3.** e **4.** h **5.** g **6.** d **7.** a **8.** f **Actividad C** **1.** c **2.** b **3.** a **4.** a
5. c **6.** c

Gramática

Actividad E **1.** a **2.** b **3.** b **4.** c **5.** b **6.** c **Actividad F** **1.** A man is calling her. **2.** My father
kisses my mother. **3.** A child is looking for her. **4.** Our parents help us. **5.** She wants to call him.
6. The children detest them.

TERCERA PARTE

Vocabulario

Actividad A **1.** d **2.** e **3.** c **4.** a **5.** f **6.** b **Actividad C** **1.** ilógico **2.** ilógico **3.** lógico **4.** lógico **5.** ilógico **6.** ilógico

Gramática

Actividad D **1.** más **2.** menos **3.** menor **4.** mayor **5.** más **6.** más **Actividad F** **1.** b **2.** a **3.** b **4.** c **5.** c **6.** c

¡A escuchar!

Después de escuchar
Paso 1 A Marisela no le gusta la actitud de Carlos. / Roberto y Marisela piensan que Carlos no trata bien a sus empleados. / Roberto cree que Jaime está preocupado. **Paso 2** **1.** no **2.** nervioso y preocupado. **3.** sí **4.** está serio y distraído **Paso 3** **1./2.** *Possible answers:* Carlos es tan mentiroso como Jaime. Un jefe no puede tratar a sus empleados igual que a su familia. Carlos es más mentiroso que Jaime. Carlos está más cansado que nervioso. Carlos es mayor que su hermana. Jaime tiene tantas preocupaciones como Carlos.

Lección 3B

PRIMERA PARTE

Vocabulario

Actividad A **1.** c **2.** d **3.** b **4.** d **5.** c **6.** d **7.** a **8.** c

Gramática

Actividad D **1.** malo **2.** bueno **3.** malo **4.** malo **5.** bueno **6.** malo **7.** malo **8.** bueno
Actividad F **1.** Siempre **2.** nada **3.** jamás **4.** ninguna **5.** También **6.** alguien

SEGUNDA PARTE

Vocabulario

Actividad A **1.** c **2.** b **3.** b **4.** a **5.** c **6.** a **Actividad C** **1.** a **2.** b **3.** c **4.** b **5.** c **6.** a

Gramática

Actividad E **1.** c **2.** b **3.** c **4.** b **5.** b **6.** c **Actividad F** **1.** está **2.** ser **3.** está **4.** son **5.** están **6.** está **7.** es

TERCERA PARTE

Vocabulario

Actividad B **1.** f **2.** e **3.** d **4.** b **5.** h **6.** a **7.** c **8.** g **Actividad C** **1.** c **2.** a **3.** b **4.** a **5.** c **6.** c **7.** b **8.** a

Gramática

Actividad E 4, 3, 6, 1, 2, 5, 7 **Actividad F** **1.** le **2.** les **3.** les **4.** le **5.** les **6.** le

Para escribir

Antes de escribir
Answers may vary. **1.** Carlos **2.** Jaime **3.** Carlos **4.** Jaime **5.** Jaime **6.** los dos **7.** los dos **8.** los dos

Lección 4A

PRIMERA PARTE

Vocabulario

Actividad B   1. d   2. h   3. e   4. a   5. c   6. g   7. b   8. f   **Actividad C**   1. cierto   2. falso   3. falso   4. cierto   5. falso   6. falso   7. falso   8. cierto

Gramática

Actividad F   1. otra persona: Leonardo da Vinci   2. yo   3. otra persona: Cristóbal Colón y otros   4. yo   5. otra persona: Neil Armstrong y otros   6. otra persona: su hermano Wilbur Wright

SEGUNDA PARTE

Vocabulario

Actividad B   1. b   2. c   3. a   4. b   5. c   6. a   7. b   8. b   **Actividad C**   1. falso   2. cierto   3. cierto   4. falso   5. cierto   6. cierto   7. cierto   8. cierto

Gramática

Actividad D   1. pretérito   2. pretérito   3. presente   4. pretérito   5. presente   6. pretérito   7. pretérito   8. presente

TERCERA PARTE

Vocabulario

Actividad B   1. S   2. N   3. S   4. N   5. S   6. S   7. N   **Actividad C**   1. b   2. c   3. c   4. b   5. a   6. c

Gramática

Actividad E   1. d   2. b   3. c   4. a   5. g   6. h   7. e   8. f

¡A escuchar!

Después de escuchar
Paso 1   que descubrió algo   **Paso 2**   1. Carlos y Jaime   2. está loca   3. Dice que Jaime trata de ser cortés con María.   4. no   **Paso 3**   *Answers will vary. Possible verbs include:* descubrí: descubrir; hubo, haber; dijo, decir; mintió, mentir; se encontraron, encontrarse; preguntó, preguntar; volvió, volver; pasó, pasar; fue, ser; hablé, hablar; dio, dar; regaló, regalar

Lección 4B

PRIMERA PARTE

Vocabulario

Actividad B   1. falso   2. cierto   3. cierto   4. cierto   5. cierto   6. cierto   7. cierto   8. falso

Gramática

Actividad C   1. f   2. e   3. b, d   4. c   5. a   **Actividad D**   1. e   2. d   3. g   4. f   5. a   6. b   7. c

Vocabulario

Actividad B **1.** falso **2.** falso **3.** cierto **4.** cierto **5.** falso **6.** cierto **7.** falso **8.** cierto

Gramática

Actividad D **1.** f **2.** c **3.** e **4.** d **5.** a **6.** b

TERCERA PARTE

Vocabulario

Actividad A **1.** d **2.** e **3.** h **4.** g **5.** b **6.** f **7.** a **8.** c **Actividad C** **1.** b **2.** a **3.** c **4.** a **5.** b **6.** b **7.** a **8.** c

Gramática

Actividad E **1.** por **2.** para **3.** para **4.** por **5.** por **6.** para **7.** por **8.** para

Para escribir

Antes de escribir
Paso 2 *Chronological order of events:* 1, 5, 2, 3, 6, 9, 10, 4, 7, 11, 8, 12

Lección 5A

PRIMERA PARTE

Vocabulario

Actividad B 5, 4, 6, 3, 2, 8, 1, 7 **Actividad C** **1.** ventaja **2.** desventaja **3.** ventaja o desventaja **4.** desventaja **5.** ventaja **6.** ventaja o desventaja **7.** desventaja **8.** ventaja

Gramática

Actividad D **1.** a **2.** b **3.** b **4.** b **5.** b **6.** a

SEGUNDA PARTE

Vocabulario

Actividad B **1.** el estéreo **2.** el teléfono **3.** el televisor y el teléfono **4.** el televisor y el teléfono **5.** el teléfono **6.** el televisor y el estéreo **7.** el televisor **Actividad C** **1.** Funciona. **2.** No funciona. **3.** No funciona. **4.** No funciona. **5.** No funciona. **6.** Funciona. **7.** Funciona. **8.** No funciona.

Gramática

Actividad E, Paso 1 **1.** b, d **2.** b, c **3.** a, d **4.** b, d **5.** a, d **Actividad F** **1.** a **2.** b **3.** b **4.** a **5.** b **6.** c **7.** b

TERCERA PARTE

Vocabulario

Actividad B **1.** sedentaria **2.** activa **3.** activa **4.** sedentaria **5.** sedentaria **6.** sedentaria **7.** activa **Actividad C** **1.** b **2.** a **3.** b **4.** c **5.** a **6.** a

Gramática

Actividad D **1.** posible **2.** mentira **3.** mentira **4.** posible **5.** mentira **6.** mentira **7.** posible **8.** posible **Actividad E** **1.** c **2.** g **3.** b **4.** e **5.** a **6.** h **7.** d **8.** f

¡A escuchar!

Después de escuchar
Paso 1 Marisela tiene una opinión negativa de Carlos. **Paso 2** **1.** falso **2.** cierto **3.** no había otra persona para hacer el trabajo. **4.** falso **Paso 3** *Possible answers* **1.** A Marisela también le gusta Jaime. **2.** A Carlos no le interesa la viña. **3.** A María y Jaime les interesa saber más del otro. **4.** A Marisela no le cae bien Carlos. **5.** A Carlos no le agrada su trabajo.

Lección 5B

PRIMERA PARTE

Vocabulario

Actividad A *Correct order indicated in parentheses.* **1.** 535.000 (6) **2.** 2.010 (2) **3.** 3.342.615 (8) **4.** 14.200 (3) **5.** 1.739 (1) **6.** 21.998 (4) **7.** 300.300 (5) **8.** 888.002 (7) **Actividad B** **1.** b, 1873 **2.** f, 1010 **3.** h, 1623 **4.** a, 1286 **5.** g, 1312 **6.** c, 2052 **7.** e, 1492 **8.** d, 1776

Gramática

Actividad C **1.** e **2.** b **3.** f **4.** a **5.** c **6.** d **Actividad E** **1.** g **2.** e **3.** f **4.** a **5.** h **6.** c **7.** d **8.** b

SEGUNDA PARTE

Vocabulario

Actividad A **1.** c **2.** b **3.** a **4.** b **5.** c **6.** c **Actividad C** **1.** d **2.** g **3.** b **4.** a **5.** e **6.** f **7.** c

Gramática

Actividad E **1.** b **2.** a **3.** b **4.** a **5.** a **6.** a

TERCERA PARTE

Vocabulario

Actividad A **1.** e **2.** c **3.** a **4.** f **5.** d **6.** b

Gramática

Actividad C **1.** distracción **2.** distracción **3.** ayuda **4.** ayuda **5.** distracción **6.** ayuda **7.** ayuda **8.** distracción

Para escribir

Antes de escribir
Paso 1 **1.** Jaime **2.** María **3.** Jaime **4.** María **5.** Jaime **6.** Jaime **7.** Jaime y María **8.** Jaime **9.** Jaime y María **10.** Jaime **11.** Jaime y María **Paso 2** *Chronological order of events (answers may vary slightly)*: 1, 2, 10, 7, 8, 5, 6, 9, 11, 4, 3

VERBS

A. Regular Verbs: Simple Tenses

INFINITIVE / PRESENT PARTICIPLE / PAST PARTICIPLE	INDICATIVE					SUBJUNCTIVE		IMPERATIVE
	PRESENT	IMPERFECT	PRETERITE	FUTURE	CONDITIONAL	PRESENT	IMPERFECT	
hablar hablando hablado	hablo hablas habla hablamos habláis hablan	hablaba hablabas hablaba hablábamos hablabais hablaban	hablé hablaste habló hablamos hablasteis hablaron	hablaré hablarás hablará hablaremos hablaréis hablarán	hablaría hablarías hablaría hablaríamos hablaríais hablarían	hable hables hable hablemos habléis hablen	hablara hablaras hablara habláramos hablarais hablaran	habla / no hables hable hablemos hablad / no habléis hablen
comer comiendo comido	como comes come comemos coméis comen	comía comías comía comíamos comíais comían	comí comiste comió comimos comisteis comieron	comeré comerás comerá comeremos comeréis comerán	comería comerías comería comeríamos comeríais comerían	coma comas coma comamos comáis coman	comiera comieras comiera comiéramos comierais comieran	come / no comas coma comamos comed / no comáis coman
vivir viviendo vivido	vivo vives vive vivimos vivís viven	vivía vivías vivía vivíamos vivíais vivían	viví viviste vivió vivimos vivisteis vivieron	viviré vivirás vivirá viviremos viviréis vivirán	viviría vivirías viviría viviríamos viviríais vivirían	viva vivas viva vivamos viváis vivan	viviera vivieras viviera viviéramos vivierais vivieran	vive / no vivas viva vivamos vivid / no viváis vivan

B. Regular Verbs: Perfect Tenses

INDICATIVE					SUBJUNCTIVE	
PRESENT PERFECT	PAST PERFECT	PRETERITE PERFECT	FUTURE PERFECT	CONDITIONAL PERFECT	PRESENT PERFECT	PAST PERFECT
he has ha hemos habéis han } hablado comido vivido	había habías había habíamos habíais habían } hablado comido vivido	hube hubiste hubo hubimos hubisteis hubieron } hablado comido vivido	habré habrás habrá habremos habréis habrán } hablado comido vivido	habría habrías habría habríamos habríais habrían } hablado comido vivido	haya hayas haya hayamos hayáis hayan } hablado comido vivido	hubiera hubieras hubiera hubiéramos hubierais hubieran } hablado comido vivido

C. Irregular Verbs

INFINITIVE PRESENT PARTICIPLE PAST PARTICIPLE	INDICATIVE					SUBJUNCTIVE		IMPERATIVE
	PRESENT	IMPERFECT	PRETERITE	FUTURE	CONDITIONAL	PRESENT	IMPERFECT	
andar andando andado	ando andas anda andamos andáis andan	andaba andabas andaba andábamos andabais andaban	anduve anduviste anduvo anduvimos anduvisteis anduvieron	andaré andarás andará andaremos andaréis andarán	andaría andarías andaría andaríamos andaríais andarían	ande andes ande andemos andéis anden	anduviera anduvieras anduviera anduviéramos anduvierais anduvieran	anda / no andes ande andemos andad / no andéis anden
caer cayendo caído	caigo caes cae caemos caéis caen	caía caías caía caíamos caíais caían	caí caíste cayó caímos caísteis cayeron	caeré caerás caerá caeremos caeréis caerán	caería caerías caería caeríamos caeríais caerían	caiga caigas caiga caigamos caigáis caigan	cayera cayeras cayera cayéramos cayerais cayeran	cae / no caigas caiga caigamos caed / no caigáis caigan
dar dando dado	doy das da damos dais dan	daba dabas daba dábamos dabais daban	di diste dio dimos disteis dieron	daré darás dará daremos daréis darán	daría darías daría daríamos daríais darían	dé des dé demos deis den	diera dieras diera diéramos dierais dieran	da / no des dé demos dad / no deis den
decir diciendo dicho	digo dices dice decimos decís dicen	decía decías decía decíamos decíais decían	dije dijiste dijo dijimos dijisteis dijeron	diré dirás dirá diremos diréis dirán	diría dirías diría diríamos diríais dirían	diga digas diga digamos digáis digan	dijera dijeras dijera dijéramos dijerais dijeran	di / no digas diga digamos decid / no digáis digan
estar estando estado	estoy estás está estamos estáis están	estaba estabas estaba estábamos estabais estaban	estuve estuviste estuvo estuvimos estuvisteis estuvieron	estaré estarás estará estaremos estaréis estarán	estaría estarías estaría estaríamos estaríais estarían	esté estés esté estemos estéis estén	estuviera estuvieras estuviera estuviéramos estuvierais estuvieran	está / no estés esté estemos estad / no estéis estén
haber habiendo habido	he has ha hemos habéis han	había habías había habíamos habíais habían	hube hubiste hubo hubimos hubisteis hubieron	habré habrás habrá habremos habréis habrán	habría habrías habría habríamos habríais habrían	haya hayas haya hayamos hayáis hayan	hubiera hubieras hubiera hubiéramos hubierais hubieran	
hacer haciendo hecho	hago haces hace hacemos hacéis hacen	hacía hacías hacía hacíamos hacíais hacían	hice hiciste hizo hicimos hicisteis hicieron	haré harás hará haremos haréis harán	haría harías haría haríamos haríais harían	haga hagas haga hagamos hagáis hagan	hiciera hicieras hiciera hiciéramos hicierais hicieran	haz / no hagas haga hagamos haced / no hagáis hagan

C. Irregular Verbs (*continued*)

INFINITIVE PRESENT PARTICIPLE PAST PARTICIPLE	INDICATIVE					SUBJUNCTIVE		IMPERATIVE
	PRESENT	IMPERFECT	PRETERITE	FUTURE	CONDITIONAL	PRESENT	IMPERFECT	
ir yendo ido	voy	iba	fui	iré	iría	vaya	fuera	
	vas	ibas	fuiste	irás	irías	vayas	fueras	ve / no vayas
	va	iba	fue	irá	iría	vaya	fuera	vaya
	vamos	íbamos	fuimos	iremos	iríamos	vayamos	fuéramos	vamos / no vayamos
	vais	ibais	fuisteis	iréis	iríais	vayáis	fuerais	id / no vayáis
	van	iban	fueron	irán	irían	vayan	fueran	vayan
oír oyendo oído	oigo	oía	oí	oiré	oiría	oiga	oyera	
	oyes	oías	oíste	oirás	oirías	oigas	oyeras	oye / no oigas
	oye	oía	oyó	oirá	oiría	oiga	oyera	oiga
	oímos	oíamos	oímos	oiremos	oiríamos	oigamos	oyéramos	oigamos
	oís	oíais	oísteis	oiréis	oiríais	oigáis	oyerais	oíd / no oigáis
	oyen	oían	oyeron	oirán	oirían	oigan	oyeran	oigan
poder pudiendo podido	puedo	podía	pude	podré	podría	pueda	pudiera	
	puedes	podías	pudiste	podrás	podrías	puedas	pudieras	
	puede	podía	pudo	podrá	podría	pueda	pudiera	
	podemos	podíamos	pudimos	podremos	podríamos	podamos	pudiéramos	
	podéis	podíais	pudisteis	podréis	podríais	podáis	pudierais	
	pueden	podían	pudieron	podrán	podrían	puedan	pudieran	
poner poniendo puesto	pongo	ponía	puse	pondré	pondría	ponga	pusiera	
	pones	ponías	pusiste	pondrás	pondrías	pongas	pusieras	pon / no pongas
	pone	ponía	puso	pondrá	pondría	ponga	pusiera	ponga
	ponemos	poníamos	pusimos	pondremos	pondríamos	pongamos	pusiéramos	pongamos
	ponéis	poníais	pusisteis	pondréis	pondríais	pongáis	pusierais	poned / no pongáis
	ponen	ponían	pusieron	pondrán	pondrían	pongan	pusieran	pongan
querer queriendo querido	quiero	quería	quise	querré	querría	quiera	quisiera	
	quieres	querías	quisiste	querrás	querrías	quieras	quisieras	quiere / no quieras
	quiere	quería	quiso	querrá	querría	quiera	quisiera	quiera
	queremos	queríamos	quisimos	querremos	querríamos	queramos	quisiéramos	queramos
	queréis	queríais	quisisteis	querréis	querríais	queráis	quisierais	quered / no queráis
	quieren	querían	quisieron	querrán	querrían	quieran	quisieran	quieran
saber sabiendo sabido	sé	sabía	supe	sabré	sabría	sepa	supiera	
	sabes	sabías	supiste	sabrás	sabrías	sepas	supieras	sabe / no sepas
	sabe	sabía	supo	sabrá	sabría	sepa	supiera	sepa
	sabemos	sabíamos	supimos	sabremos	sabríamos	sepamos	supiéramos	sepamos
	sabéis	sabíais	supisteis	sabréis	sabríais	sepáis	supierais	sabed / no sepáis
	saben	sabían	supieron	sabrán	sabrían	sepan	supieran	sepan
salir saliendo salido	salgo	salía	salí	saldré	saldría	salga	saliera	
	sales	salías	saliste	saldrás	saldrías	salgas	salieras	sal / no salgas
	sale	salía	salió	saldrá	saldría	salga	saliera	salga
	salimos	salíamos	salimos	saldremos	saldríamos	salgamos	saliéramos	salgamos
	salís	salíais	salisteis	saldréis	saldríais	salgáis	salierais	salid / no salgáis
	salen	salían	salieron	saldrán	saldrían	salgan	salieran	salgan

C. Irregular Verbs (*continued*)

INFINITIVE PRESENT PARTICIPLE PAST PARTICIPLE	INDICATIVE					SUBJUNCTIVE		IMPERATIVE
	PRESENT	IMPERFECT	PRETERITE	FUTURE	CONDITIONAL	PRESENT	IMPERFECT	
ser siendo sido	soy eres es somos sois son	era eras era éramos erais eran	fui fuiste fue fuimos fuisteis fueron	seré serás será seremos seréis serán	sería serías sería seríamos seríais serían	sea seas sea seamos seáis sean	fuera fueras fuera fuéramos fuerais fueran	sé / no seas sea seamos sed / no seáis sean
tener teniendo tenido	tengo tienes tiene tenemos tenéis tienen	tenía tenías tenía teníamos teníais tenían	tuve tuviste tuvo tuvimos tuvisteis tuvieron	tendré tendrás tendrá tendremos tendréis tendrán	tendría tendrías tendría tendríamos tendríais tendrían	tenga tengas tenga tengamos tengáis tengan	tuviera tuvieras tuviera tuviéramos tuvierais tuvieran	ten / no tengas tenga tengamos tened / no tengáis tengan
traer trayendo traído	traigo traes trae traemos traéis traen	traía traías traía traíamos traíais traían	traje trajiste trajo trajimos trajisteis trajeron	traeré traerás traerá traeremos traeréis traerán	traería traerías traería traeríamos traeríais traerían	traiga traigas traiga traigamos traigáis traigan	trajera trajeras trajera trajéramos trajerais trajeran	trae / no traigas traiga traigamos traed / no traigáis traigan
venir viniendo venido	vengo vienes viene venimos venís vienen	venía venías venía veníamos veníais venían	vine viniste vino vinimos vinisteis vinieron	vendré vendrás vendrá vendremos vendréis vendrán	vendría vendrías vendría vendríamos vendríais vendrían	venga vengas venga vengamos vengáis vengan	viniera vinieras viniera viniéramos vinierais vinieran	ven / no vengas venga vengamos venid / no vengáis vengan
ver viendo visto	veo ves ve vemos veis ven	veía veías veía veíamos veíais veían	vi viste vio vimos visteis vieron	veré verás verá veremos veréis verán	vería verías vería veríamos veríais verían	vea veas vea veamos veáis vean	viera vieras viera viéramos vierais vieran	ve / no veas vea veamos ved / no veáis vean

D. Stem-Changing and Spelling Change Verbs

INFINITIVE PRESENT PARTICIPLE PAST PARTICIPLE	INDICATIVE					SUBJUNCTIVE		IMPERATIVE
	PRESENT	IMPERFECT	PRETERITE	FUTURE	CONDITIONAL	PRESENT	IMPERFECT	
construir (y) construyendo construido	construyo construyes construye construimos construís construyen	construía construías construía construíamos construíais construían	construí construiste construyó construimos construisteis construyeron	construiré construirás construirá construiremos construiréis construirán	construiría construirías construiría construiríamos construiríais construirían	construya construyas construya construyamos construyáis construyan	construyera construyeras construyera construyéramos construyerais construyeran	construye / no construyas construya construyamos construid / no construyáis construyan
dormir (ue, u) durmiendo dormido	duermo duermes duerme dormimos dormís duermen	dormía dormías dormía dormíamos dormíais dormían	dormí dormiste durmió dormimos dormisteis durmieron	dormiré dormirás dormirá dormiremos dormiréis dormirán	dormiría dormirías dormiría dormiríamos dormiríais dormirían	duerma duermas duerma durmamos durmáis duerman	durmiera durmieras durmiera durmiéramos durmierais durmieran	duerme / no duermas duerma durmamos dormid / no durmáis duerman

D. Stem-Changing and Spelling Change Verbs (continued)

INFINITIVE PRESENT PARTICIPLE PAST PARTICIPLE	INDICATIVE					SUBJUNCTIVE		IMPERATIVE
	PRESENT	IMPERFECT	PRETERITE	FUTURE	CONDITIONAL	PRESENT	IMPERFECT	
pedir (i, i) pidiendo pedido	pido pides pide pedimos pedís piden	pedía pedías pedía pedíamos pedíais pedían	pedí pediste pidió pedimos pedisteis pidieron	pediré pedirás pedirá pediremos pediréis pedirán	pediría pedirías pediría pediríamos pediríais pedirían	pida pidas pida pidamos pidáis pidan	pidiera pidieras pidiera pidiéramos pidierais pidieran	pide / no pidas pida pidamos pedid / no pidáis pidan
pensar (ie) pensando pensado	pienso piensas piensa pensamos pensáis piensan	pensaba pensabas pensaba pensábamos pensabais pensaban	pensé pensaste pensó pensamos pensasteis pensaron	pensaré pensarás pensará pensaremos pensaréis pensarán	pensaría pensarías pensaría pensaríamos pensaríais pensarían	piense pienses piense pensemos penséis piensen	pensara pensaras pensara pensáramos pensarais pensaran	piensa / no pienses piense pensemos pensad / no penséis piensen
producir (zc) produciendo producido	produzco produces produce producimos producís producen	producía producías producía producíamos producíais producían	produje produjiste produjo produjimos produjisteis produjeron	produciré producirás producirá produciremos produciréis producirán	produciría producirías produciría produciríamos produciríais producirían	produzca produzcas produzca produzcamos produzcáis produzcan	produjera produjeras produjera produjéramos produjerais produjeran	produce / no produzcas produzca produzcamos producid / no produzcáis produzcan
reír (i, i) riendo reído	río ríes ríe reímos reís ríen	reía reías reía reíamos reíais reían	reí reíste rió reímos reísteis rieron	reiré reirás reirá reiremos reiréis reirán	reiría reirías reiría reiríamos reiríais reirían	ría rías ría riamos riáis rían	riera rieras riera riéramos rierais rieran	ríe / no rías ría riamos reíd / no riáis rían
seguir (i, i) (g) siguiendo seguido	sigo sigues sigue seguimos seguís siguen	seguía seguías seguía seguíamos seguíais seguían	seguí seguiste siguió seguimos seguisteis siguieron	seguiré seguirás seguirá seguiremos seguiréis seguirán	seguiría seguirías seguiría seguiríamos seguiríais seguirían	siga sigas siga sigamos sigáis sigan	siguiera siguieras siguiera siguiéramos siguierais siguieran	sigue / no sigas siga sigamos seguid / no sigáis sigan
sentir (ie, i) sintiendo sentido	siento sientes siente sentimos sentís sienten	sentía sentías sentía sentíamos sentíais sentían	sentí sentiste sintió sentimos sentisteis sintieron	sentiré sentirás sentirá sentiremos sentiréis sentirán	sentiría sentirías sentiría sentiríamos sentiríais sentirían	sienta sientas sienta sintamos sintáis sientan	sintiera sintieras sintiera sintiéramos sintierais sintieran	siente / no sientas sienta sintamos sentid / no sintáis sientan
volver (ue) volviendo vuelto	vuelvo vuelves vuelve volvemos volvéis vuelven	volvía volvías volvía volvíamos volvíais volvían	volví volviste volvió volvimos volvisteis volvieron	volveré volverás volverá volveremos volveréis volverán	volvería volverías volvería volveríamos volveríais volverían	vuelva vuelvas vuelva volvamos volváis vuelvan	volviera volvieras volviera volviéramos volvierais volvieran	vuelve / no vuelvas vuelva volvamos volved / no volváis vuelvan

ABOUT THE AUTHORS

BILL VANPATTEN is Professor of Spanish and Second Language Acquisition at the University of Illinois at Chicago where he is also the Director of Spanish Basic Language. His areas of research are input and input processing in second language acquisition and the effects of formal instruction on acquisitional processes. He has published widely in the fields of second language acquisition and language teaching and is a frequent conference speaker and presenter. In addition to *Sol y viento*, he is also the lead author of *¿Sabías que... ?*, Fourth Edition (2004, McGraw-Hill) and *Vistazos*, Second Edition (2006, McGraw-Hill). He is also the lead author and designer of *Destinos* and co-author with James F. Lee of *Making Communicative Language Teaching Happen*, Second Edition (2003, McGraw-Hill). He is also the author of *Input Processing and Grammar Instruction: Theory and Research* (1996, Ablex/Greenwood) and *From Input to Output: A Teacher's Guide to Second Language Acquisition* (2003, McGraw-Hill), and he is the editor of *Processing Instruction: Theory, Research, and Commentary* (2004, Erlbaum). When not engaged in academic activities, he writes fiction and performs stand-up comedy.

MICHAEL J. LEESER is Assistant Professor of Spanish in the Department of Modern Languages and Linguistics at Florida State University, where he is also Director of the Spanish Basic Language Program. Before joining the faculty at Florida State, he taught a wide range of courses at the secondary and postsecondary levels, including courses in Spanish language and Hispanic cultures, teacher preparation courses for secondary school teachers, and graduate courses in communicative language teaching and second language acquisition. He received his Ph.D. in Spanish (Second Language Acquisition and Teacher Education) from the University of Illinois at Urbana-Champaign in 2003. His research interests include input processing during second language reading as well as second language classroom interaction. His research has appeared in journals such as *Studies in Second Language Acquisition* and *Language Teaching Research*. He also co-authored the CD-ROM, along with Bill VanPatten and Mark Overstreet, for *¿Sabías que... ?*, Fourth Edition (2004, McGraw-Hill).

GREGORY D. KEATING will complete his Ph.D. in Hispanic Linguistics and Second Language Acquisition at the University of Illinois at Chicago in 2005. His areas of research include Spanish sentence processing, the role instruction plays in language acquisition, and the acquisition of Spanish syntax and vocabulary. His doctoral research explores the relationship between language processing and grammatical competence in the acquisition of Spanish gender agreement. He is a frequent presenter at conferences in the United States and Mexico. He is also a recipient of several teaching awards, including one from the University of Notre Dame, where he received his M.A. in Spanish Literature. In addition to teaching and research, he has supervised many language courses and teaching assistants and has assisted in the coordination of technology-enhanced lower division Spanish language programs.

TONY HOUSTON is Assistant Professor of Spanish at Saint Louis University, where he teaches Spanish language, applied linguistics, and teaching methods and where he serves as Coordinator of Basic and Intermediate Spanish. He earned his Ph.D. in Spanish and Second Language Acquisition and Teacher Education at the University of Illinois at Urbana-Champaign in 1996. His research interests include input processing, classroom discourse, and outcomes assessment, as well as applications of learning theory to language instruction. He has authored articles on the role of context and background knowledge in sentence processing, classroom communication strategies, outcomes assessment and mindful learning. He has developed WebCT materials for the Intermediate Spanish textbook *¿Qué te parece?*, Second Edition (2000, McGraw-Hill). He was a collaborative assistant on the revisions to the second edition of Sandra J. Savignon's book *Communicative Competence: Theory and Classroom Practice* (1997, McGraw-Hill) for the McGraw-Hill Second Language Professional Series.